A Rauschenbusch Reader

A

Rauschenbusch Reader

The Kingdom of God and

the Social Gospel

COMPILED BY BENSON Y. LANDIS

With an Interpretation of the Life and
Work of Walter Rauschenbusch
by Harry Emerson Fosdick

H|B

HARPER & BROTHERS PUBLISHERS, NEW YORK

Library of Congress catalog card number: 57-7351

CONTENTS

PREFACE   vii

ACKNOWLEDGMENT   xi

INTRODUCTION, by Harry Emerson Fosdick   xiii

   I   CHRISTIANITY AND THE SOCIAL CRISIS   1

        The Historical Roots of Christianity
        The Social Aims of Jesus
        The Social Impetus of Primitive Christianity
        Why Has Christianity Never Undertaken the Work of
           Social Reconstruction?
        The Present Crisis
        The Stake of the Church in the Social Movement
        What to Do

  II   THE SOCIAL MEANING OF THE LORD'S PRAYER   30

 III   CHRISTIANIZING THE SOCIAL ORDER   37

        Wanted: A Faith for a Task
        "The Powers of the Coming Age"
        The Revival of Religion and the Conversion of the
           Strong

  IV   A SOCIAL LITANY   73

   V   DARE WE BE CHRISTIANS?   76

  VI   THE SOCIAL PRINCIPLES OF JESUS   89

 VII   A THEOLOGY FOR THE SOCIAL GOSPEL   102

        The Challenge of the Social Gospel to Theology
        The Kingdom of God
        The Social Gospel and the Conception of God

VIII   CONTRIBUTIONS TO THE BAPTIST CONGRESS   128

      The Church and the Money Power
      Ethical *versus* Forensic Conceptions of Salvation
      The Lessons of Economic History
      On Monopolies
      The Interpenetration of the Life of Church and State
      The Pulpit in Relation to Political and Social Reform

  IX   THE LITTLE GATE TO GOD   148

   X   AN AFFIRMATION OF FAITH   149

  XI   PRAYERS OF THE SOCIAL AWAKENING   150

 XII   A LETTER TO ONE ENTERING THE MINISTRY   162

A CHRONOLOGY   163

INDEX   165

PREFACE

This Reader presents a selection of the writings from the pen of a modern prophet. I have endeavored to arrange a fair representation of the voluminous writings of Walter Rauschenbusch. The immediate occasion for the compilation of this Reader is the recognition in 1957 of the fiftieth anniversary of the publication of Rauschenbusch's first major work, *Christianity and the Social Crisis*.

More than half of this Reader contains large portions of three books: *Christianity and the Social Crisis*, *Christianizing the Social Order* (1912), and *A Theology for the Social Gospel* (1917). Much of the message of this great and good man is found in these books. Adequate quotations are also taken from the book, *The Social Principles of Jesus* (1916), and from a booklet, *Dare We Be Christians* (1914). A *Social Litany* is printed in full.

Before every chapter appear explanations of the source and the context of the selections that are published. The quotations are, in general, fairly lengthy sections of the writings. In a number of instances, however, it has been necessary to abridge paragraphs and combine them. In all such cases, the words are those of Walter Rauschenbusch. Probably some of the users of this Reader will wish to consult the full text of the original works.

The writings on devotion and personal faith are generously quoted in order to illustrate the scope of Rauschenbusch's writings on both a personal and a social gospel. Accordingly a number of the prayers first published in the United States in a collection in 1910 are given in full. A further range is provided by printing various contributions by Rauschenbusch to the sessions of the Baptist Congress for the discussion of current questions between the years 1889 and 1898.

The works of this writer of power are permitted in this compilation to speak for themselves in all their vitality, their freshness, and their amazingly current implications many years after they were written. Accordingly, the compiler's notes are as brief as possible, being made only for the purpose of identification of the materials, and of their setting, or of maintaining a continuity in the selections.

It is frankly recognized by this compiler that Rauschenbusch wrote many works not quoted here. It was decided to quote somewhat generously from definitely limited sources rather than to refer more briefly to more titles. The main drives of this prophetic writer are believed to be given here. At least the compiler professes to have been no censor but to have permitted a free flow from Rauschenbusch to the modern reader and student.

Dr. Fosdick's personal interpretation of the life and work of Walter Rauschenbusch appropriately rounds out this anthology. As a further aid, a chronology has been compiled. For a complete biography, reference may be made to *Walter Rauschenbusch* by Dores Robinson Sharpe (New York, 1942). The now numerous Rauschenbusch lectures contain further interpretations and tributes.

Rauschenbusch wrote his first major work in an era marked by considerable excitement and a ferment of public discussion over national policies. Theodore Roosevelt, who later sought Rauschenbusch's counsel, was brandishing a big stick as he dealt with exploiters of lands and resources, and with tendencies toward monopoly on the part of rapidly growing and powerful corporations. Mr. Roosevelt wished to make the Republican party an effective instrument of progressive public policies in opposition to the standpatters of his day. Mr. Roosevelt was one of the most discussed and one of the most popular of presidents. He was once described as the favorite author of the American farmers.

William Jennings Bryan, spokesman of the people of the prairies, wished in the early twentieth century to reorganize the Democratic party. He strove to make it a more "radical" party than it had been. He frequently used the word radical and was unafraid of it. He had come to national prominence as a young man in 1896 with his now famous "cross-of-gold" speech at the Democratic National Convention, which then nominated him as its candidate. This spokesman of "populist" policies contributed to the era of national controversy over social and economic policies and the role of the Government.

The Protestant churches, to which the Prophet of Rochester addressed much of his thunder, were in the grip of traditional individualism. The personal piety of the early years of the nation was still the dominant note. The churches were interested in conventional foreign missions—"the evangelization of the world in this generation." Their home missionaries followed the people into the new territories such as Oklahoma and Arizona, which had not yet become states. The churches ran evangelistic campaigns. They conducted Sunday schools, taught temperance, and had two church services a Sunday. They opposed dancing. They saw sin as associated largely with sex, and did not consider organized economic forces as particularly evil. Theirs was an easy blend of piety, secular optimism, and patriotism. Their social activities were largely in the form of simple acts of service that displeased no one in particular. Their religious expressions were simple and vague. They thought they saw simple causes of various phenomena in a relatively simple society.

Into this individualism and complacency came the strong voice of a professor in a theological seminary who was as much surprised as anyone when he found himself discussed everywhere and in demand as a lecturer and writer. What he taught and wrote is at least well illustrated in this Reader, along with compiler's notes concerning the situation in the years when his major works appeared.

BENSON Y. LANDIS

ACKNOWLEDGMENT

This selection of readings is published by permission of the sons and daughters of Walter Rauschenbusch. The compiler gratefully records his acknowledgment to them.

The following publishers have also granted permissions: The Pilgrim Press, for *Dare We Be Christians* and *Prayers of the Social Awakening*; Association Press, for *The Social Principles of Jesus*; The Macmillan Company, for *Christianizing the Social Order* and *A Theology for the Social Gospel*.

INTRODUCTION

An Interpretation of the Life and Work
of Walter Rauschenbusch

BY HARRY EMERSON FOSDICK

Fifty years ago Walter Rauschenbusch, a professor in the Rochester Theological Seminary, Rochester, New York, handed the manuscript of a book to his publisher and took ship for a year's study in Germany. When he returned he found that the book had made him one of the most renowned and influential personalities in the American churches. That was not what he had expected. "This was a dangerous book," he said later, "and I entered upon my task with fear and trembling." Apparently he even thought that the Seminary might not retain him on its faculty. "I eagerly watched the first newspaper comments on it," he wrote, "and to my great astonishment everybody was kind to it. Only a few 'damned' it."

Reading *Christianity and the Social Crisis* today, one shares the author's surprise at its reception. It was a dangerous book—a forthright, hard-hitting, prophetic utterance, stern in its attack on the social evils of that era and on the Church's failures in dealing with them. Severe in its diagnosis and radical in its prescriptions, it inevitably aroused controversy, but the wonder is that it struck home so poignantly on the intelligence and conscience of the churches that it ushered in a new era in Christian thought and action.

Walter Rauschenbusch became in his time an outstanding personality; "the greatest single personal influence on the life and thought of the American Church in the last fifty years," so one distinguished churchman described him. To those of us who knew Rauschenbusch, who saw at first hand the social and economic conditions at the turn of the century, and who felt directly the impact of his influence, he is a vivid figure. Now, however, his books—*Christianity and the Social Crisis, Christianizing the Social Order, Prayers of the Social Awakening, A Theology for the Social Gospel*, and others—honored though they are in historical recollection, are not by many read and studied. This Reader is an endeavor to give to the new generation the gist and meat of them.

Rauschenbusch's writings, however, cannot be well understood without understanding Rauschenbusch. What put his message over was in large measure the man himself—his dynamic personality, his prophetic passion, his combined humility and courage, his profound understanding and experience of the Christian gospel, his dedicated care for people who were being hurt, exploited, and degraded by the evils of the social order, and his identification with the social revolt which in the Christian churches of the early twentieth century was urgently needing a voice to speak for it.

This Introduction is an attempt in a brief statement to make the personality of Walter Rauschenbusch come alive again in the imagination of this new generation.

Rauschenbusch was born in 1861, seven years after his father and mother had migrated from Germany to the United States. His father, who had broken with the family's Lutheran tradition and had become a Baptist, was the sixth in a direct line of clergymen. He came to America as a missionary to the German emigrants here, but his scholarship opened the way to a professorship in the Rochester Theological Seminary's German Department, where he taught for thirty years.

Into this scholarly tradition Walter was born. Throughout his youth he studied assiduously both in this country and in Germany, mastering Latin, Greek, French, German, and Hebrew, until he even wrote letters to his family not only in German and English but in Greek and Latin. At the age of seventeen his life's direction was determined by a profound religious experience, a conversion that, as he said, "influenced my soul down to its depths," and he decided to become a minister. After his graduation from the Seminary the American Baptist Foreign Mission Society almost sent him to an important educational post in India, but one of his professors at Rochester, disturbed by his liberal views about the Old Testament, blocked the appointment. During his Seminary days he had spent two summers in pastoral service in a small German Baptist Church in Kentucky, where his desire "to preach and save souls" had found satisfaction. Not unwillingly, therefore, he turned to the pastorate and in his twenty-fifth year accepted a call from the Second German Baptist Church in New York City.

This small congregation of one hundred and twenty-five members, paying their minister nine hundred dollars a year, was situated on the edge of Hell's Kitchen, one of the City's notorious slums. There Rauschenbusch saw at first hand the soul-destroying effects of destitution, overcrowded, crime-breeding tenements, and economic exploitation. For eleven years he carried on his ministry in Hell's Kitchen, and there was born the Walter Rauschenbusch who later challenged the American churches with his prophetic declaration of the social gospel.

In the middle 1880's, when Rauschenbusch began his ministry, American churches were predominantly individualistic in their emphasis. Sin and salvation were private concerns to be dealt with between the single soul and God in preparation for the final judgment and its aftermath. Social sin and social salvation were peripheral ideas when they were present at all. As Rauschenbusch said about his own early religious experience, "It had no social expression in it." Movements of protest and revolt against public evils were actively afoot, but they were almost altogether outside the churches and, like Marxian socialism, were commonly antichurch and antireligion. The field was pretty much divided then between "unsocial Christians and unchristian Socialists."

Only those who lived in the late nineteenth century can easily conceive to what lengths the individualistic emphasis in the churches went. Many believed that Christ's second coming was imminent, that until he came the world was doomed to grow continually worse, and that meanwhile man could do nothing about it. Even without such premillennial eschatology the churches' attention was centered not on seeing to it that the will of God was done on earth as it is in heaven but on seeing to it that individuals were prepared to escape from earth to the joys of heaven. As one prominent churchman put it as late as 1911: "The real business of the Church is to preach the Gospel. It is not the mission of the Church to abolish physical misery or to help men to earthly happiness." Granted the measureless service rendered to society by Christian character and Christian charity! Granted the pioneers who were courageously insisting on the application of Christian principles to business, politics, and social problems in general! Nevertheless, an individualistic otherworldliness dominated the thinking of the churches—their preaching, their programs, their theology, their evangelistic appeals.

Into this tradition Walter Rauschenbusch had been born. This was the background of his thinking when he entered the ministry. And then for eleven years he confronted Hell's Kitchen. Out of this experience came his prophetic passion for social reform. It "did not come from the Church," he said. "It came from outside. It came through personal contact with poverty, and when I saw how men toiled all their life long, hard, toilsome lives, and at the end had almost nothing to show for it; how strong men begged for work and could not get it in hard times; how little children died—oh, the children's funerals! They gripped my heart."

Because Rauschenbusch was a scholar he could not be content simply to be a social servant in Hell's Kitchen. This second conversion of his demanded the radical reconstruction of his theology, his interpretation of the Bible, and his concept of the Church's function. This reconstruction was centered in his conviction that the Kingdom of God on earth is the predominant factor in Jesus' message; that devotion to the coming of that Kingdom is the Church's all-inclusive mission; and that Christian thinking must "give it a central place and revise all other doctrines so that they will articulate organically with it." This Reign of God in a redeemed society became the focus of Rauschenbusch's thought and the passion of his life. "Here was something so big," he wrote, "that absolutely nothing that interested me was excluded from it." Personal religion, world-wide missions, justice for the workingman, the cleansing of politics, and the reformation of the economic order were all included.

To be sure, he had difficulties, which he never satisfactorily solved, in harmonizing his concept of the Kingdom with the eschatology of the New Testament. He believed in evolution; he accepted gradualism as the method of the Kingdom's coming; he rejected the idea of the sudden, catastrophic arrival of the Messiah and his reign on earth. Here, as elsewhere, he felt free to break away from ancient forms of thought which he was sure had been outgrown. He deplored the effect of pre-millennial ideas. They have allowed the Kingdom, he said, "to lead a decrepit, bed-ridden and senile existence in that museum of antiquities which we call eschatology." To him, the Kingdom was here now, as well as in the future, and to have faith in its possibility, and to further it with dedicated lives, until in justice and good will God reigns in all human affairs, was for him the very heart of Christianity.

He was not blind to the limitations involved in thus centering hope predominantly on an earthly society. The earth is not permanent. "Our race will come to an end in due time," he wrote. "The astronomical clock is already ticking which will ring in the end." Nevertheless, he returned again and again to the Master's prayer: "Thy Kingdom come; Thy will be done on earth. . . ." That was worth believing in, worth living and dying for, although the complete fulfillment of God's purpose must lie beyond earthly history, and for the individual immortality still remained the final hope.

So Rauschenbusch reoriented his thinking and his practical ministry. "Our inherited Christian faith dealt with individuals," he said. "Our present task deals with society." To be sure, he was not a lone spokes-man for this new emphasis. Men like Washington Gladden, Josiah Strong, and Richard T. Ely, to whom he paid special tribute, were blazing the trail. But, as he said, "All whose recollection runs back of 1900 will remember *that* as a time of lonesomeness. We were few and we shouted in a wilderness."

As for his parish work, he expended himself with tireless dedication in the service of individuals. Despite his attack on the old "individualism," it was to persons one by one that his major interest and devotion were given. It was because he identified himself with persons that he cared so intensely about what an evil social order was doing to them. It was because personality was to him the supreme treasure that he wanted so passionately a juster, more co-operative society which would help fulfill personality's possiblities. So for him personal and social Christianity were blended; they were one gospel indivisible. When he attacked corrupt politics, teamed up with Jacob Riis to secure playgrounds, fresh-air centers, decent housing, helped organize The Brotherhood of the Kingdom to give voice to the Christian revolt against social wrongs, and in sermons, lectures, articles pleaded for a more socialized, co-operative economic order as against the cut-throat, laissez-faire competition which then prevailed, he counted himself as much a Christian evangelist as when he proclaimed to individuals, "Ye must be born again." One of his rewards was the testimony of a butcher in Hell's Kitchen: "We have found in him more that is Christlike than in any human being we have ever met."

Then in 1897 a call came from the Rochester Theological Seminary to teach—first in the German Department and five years later in the English Department, as professor of church history. He accepted. This new relationship meant for him both a platform from which he could reach a wider audience with his social message, and an opportunity to share with new leaders of the Church the insights and convictions which he had won during the laborious years in Hell's Kitchen.

For twenty-one years, as a professor in Rochester, Rauschenbusch wielded a profound influence in his crowded classrooms. His success as a teacher was a tribute not only to his scholarship and his dynamic personality but to his patient courage, for complete deafness had be-fallen him early in his New York ministry and for the last thirty years of his life he handled that limitation with such admirable fortitude, skill, and good humor that it became an asset as well as a disadvantage. Rauschenbusch was a scholar who had become a social reformer and in his classroom both factors played powerfully on his students. They did not necessarily accept all the economic remedies which he pre-scribed—Henry George's single tax, for example—but they went out into their ministries vitally concerned about the salvation of society, as well as the regeneration of individuals.

It was through his books, however, that he most influentially reached the churches. The books were written with painstaking scholarship, but they were free from academic jargon; their style was concise, pithy, picturesque; homely metaphors and similes lighted up what else might be obscure; and the personal impact of the writer could be felt as though he were speaking directly to the reader. Deploring the concentration of wealth in a few hands, he wrote: "Wealth is to a nation what manure is to a farm. If the farmer spreads it evenly over the soil, it will enrich the whole. If he should leave it in heaps, the land would be impoverished and under the rich heaps the vegetation would be killed." Rebuking those who take for granted an unjust economic system and merely try to salvage the individual wreckage, he told of a "test applied by the head of an insane asylum to distinguish the sane from the insane. He took them to a basin of water under a running faucet and asked them to dip out the water. The insane merely dipped and dipped. The sane turned off the faucet and dipped out the rest." When Rauschenbusch wrote his books he intended that they should be read, and he succeeded.

One major factor in the influence of Rauschenbusch's writings, espe-cially within the evangelical churches, was the balance he preserved between his new emphases and the truth in the old emphases. Some enthusiasts for the social gospel put all the blame for human evil on society; change the environment and all problems will be solved, they seemed to say. But Rauschenbusch knew better. He believed in the abiding truth that underlay the old doctrine of original sin. Something is fundamentally wrong in human nature and no change of environment alone can dispense with the necessity of personal regeneration. He deplored the exclusive blaming of environment for all human evil, which attitude, he said, "instead of stiffening and awakening the sense of responsibility in the individual, teaches him to unload it on society."

While, therefore, he proclaimed the necessity of social change as vigorously as did the extreme environmentalists, he just as vigorously proclaimed the necessity of personal reformation and rebirth. "Spiritual regeneration is the most important fact in any life history," he said. "Most of the social reformers," he wrote, "claim that if only poverty and the fear of poverty could be abolished, men would cease to be grasping, selfish, overbearing and sensual. We do not see it so. . . . We can conceive of a state of society in which plenty would reign, but where universal opulence would only breed universal pride and wantonness."

This refusal of Rauschenbusch to be victimized by an either-or, when the truth lies in a both-and, is typical of him. Personal rebirth and social rebirth are inseparably necessary. One involves the other. "The social order cannot be saved," he said, "without regenerate men."

It was this quality of balanced thinking in Rauschenbusch which made multitudes of evangelical Christians listen to him, even when they did not wish to. He was not just another social reformer. He was a thoroughgoing Christian who was proclaiming the gospel.

In Rauschenbusch's lifetime it was especially difficult to keep one's thinking fairly balanced between optimism and realism. In view of two world wars and their catastrophic aftermath, Rauschenbusch, were he living now, would probably acknowledge that he did not always succeed in maintaining that balance. He certainly would not write today such sentences as this: "The largest and hardest part of the work of christianizing the social order has been done." Nevertheless, he kept his utopian hopes and his realistic appraisal of human evil in much better equilibrium than did most of his contemporaries in the field of social reform.

His was an optimistic era. Ideas of inevitable progress were in the air. Evolution was commonly interpreted not only as a biological fact but as a cosmic guarantee of inescapable social advancement "onward and upward forever." Moreover, science was implementing such hope and that entire generation was infected with it. Of course, Rauschenbusch did not altogether escape. He saw his social ideals moving forward to their consummation "with quiet march like the growing splendor of the rising sun in the East." He even said that if the men and women of his generation should become "thoroughgoing Christians, there is absolutely no question that inside of five years our social order might be transformed."

Such outbursts of fanciful hope, however, were rare and the recognized possibility of social doom gave to Rauschenbusch's thought a realistic quality that social reformers in his day commonly lacked. "The continents are strewn," he wrote, "with the ruins of dead nations and civilizations. History laughs at the optimistic illusion that 'nothing can stand in the way of human progress.' It would be safer to assert that progress is always for a time only, and then succumbs to the inevitable decay. . . . What guarantee have we, then, that our modern civilization with its pomp will not be 'one with Nineveh and Tyre'?"

The central reason for this realistic note which underlay Rauschenbusch's buoyant, enthusiastic, inspiriting call to social reform was his profound insight into the meaning of sin. The personal gospel demanded conviction of sin and genuine contrition. So, too, said Rauschenbusch, does the social gospel. It is no easy escalator, promising swift

ascent to a utopian society. It is a stern confrontation of mankind with
the scandalous, demonic evils of society—its needless poverty, brutality,
depravity, greed—and that gospel's first and indispensable effect is not
to make us cheerful optimists but, as Rauschenbusch said, to plunge
us into "a new baptism of repentance."

He was no utopian dreamer. "It rests upon us," he wrote, "to decide
if a new era is to dawn in the transformation of the world into the
Kingdom of God, or if Western civilization is to descend to the graveyard of dead civilizations, and God will have to try once more."

Present-day readers of Rauschenbusch's books are likely to have their
greatest difficulty with some of his specific economic remedies. He called
himself a Christian Socialist. Along with many American churchmen,
deeply concerned about the unjust and often cruel aspects of uncon-
trolled, competitive capitalism at the turn of the century, he saw in
socialism the implementation of his hopes. Words, however, change
their meaning. In those days Rauschenbusch could use even the word
"communism" in a Christian sense, meaning co-operativeness, collective
sharing, and good will, illustrated in the solidarity of a fine family. Of
the home, the school, and the church, he said, "These three are communistic institutions." He could say that with no prevision of the
menacing significance which half a century later communism was to
acquire. Similarly, when he called himself a "socialist," the word had
a far more flexible meaning than it has today.

Rauschenbusch never joined the Socialist party. He vigorously attacked Karl Marx and his disciples—their atheism, their materialism,
their revolutionary methods, their rigid dogmatism, their reliance on
autocratic party discipline. "The ideal of the Kingdom of God," he said,
"is not identified with any special social theory. It means justice, freedom, fraternity, labor, joy. Let each social system and movement show
us what it can contribute, and we will weigh its claims."

Indeed, in moments of prophetic foresight he feared the possible results of socialism's victory which, in one form or another, he believed
was coming. Would it be a "freshening gale" or a "typhoon"?—he was
not sure. Could he have foreseen Russian communism his direst ap-
prehensions would have been fulfilled. Meanwhile, what he meant by
socialism included a wide range of reforms which today we take for
granted: the organization of labor, income and inheritance taxes, parcel
post, cheaper postal money orders, better housing sponsored by the community, pensions for the aged, social insurance, pure food and drug laws,
limitation of the hours of labor especially for women and children, the
establishment of minimum wages, and laws condemning unsanitary and

dangerous conditions in factories. Once President Theodore Roosevelt consulted Rauschenbusch about his party's social program and Rauschenbusch expressed his belief that in one form or another socialism was coming in the United States. "Not so long as I am President," exclaimed Roosevelt, "for I will sail the ship of state alongside the ship of socialism and I will take over everything that is good in socialism and leave the bad. What will socialism do then?" Rauschenbusch laughed and answered: "I suppose the ship of socialism will sink, but that is no matter if you really save her valuable cargo."

This was his characteristic attitude. "The socialist parties," he wrote, "their technical terms, and their fighting dogmas will pass away into ancient history when their work is done. The only thing that will last and the only thing that matters is the Reign of God in humanity, and the Reign of God is vaster and higher than socialism." Nevertheless, he was a socialist. While he agreed with his fellows in the Christian Socialist Society that "as a body, we see no need now of committing ourselves to socialism in the sense of any specific system of economic doctrine," he did hold specific socialist doctrines. He believed in government ownership of coal mines and other natural resources, public ownership of railroads, water ways, gas and electric power, telegraph and telephone lines; and against laissez-faire capitalism, which in the late nineteenth century was at its cruel worst, his attacks were unrelenting and vehement. In view of all that has happened in recent decades—Russian communism, the rise and fall of totalitarian states, the radical changes in American capitalism, the amazing growth of organized labor, and the increasing recognition of government's responsibility for the welfare of all the people—one wonders how much rethinking and rewriting Rauschenbusch would feel required to do, were he alive today.

Rauschenbusch died in 1918, his final years darkly shadowed by the first World War. When the conflict began in 1914 he put crepe on the lapel of his coat and said he would keep it there until the war was finished. He was not an absolute pacifist but, as he wrote to a friend, he thought that "war is the most sinful thing there is."

To be sure, his faith was too deeply founded to be shaken by the catastrophe, despite the inexpressible disappointment it brought to his social hopes. As death drew near he wrote: "Since 1914 the world is full of hate, and I cannot expect to be happy again in my lifetime." Nevertheless, he confronted the war not as a disaster only but as a challenge, seeing in it no overthrow of the social gospel but a summons to its reaffirmation and its enlargement into the international arena.

So he fell on sleep, undefeated, undiscouraged, unashamed. He had fought a good fight and had kept the faith.

Rauschenbusch, as an individual, was a charming and forceful personality, but the extraordinary influence which he had on his generation came from more than his personal gifts. He did not speak for himself alone; he was the voice of his generation's Christian protest against the evils of an industrialized society which nineteenth-century capitalism was powerless to remedy. "This book," he wrote in one of his volumes, "is doomed to futility if it has only the personal ideas of the author behind it. It is worthy of consideration only if the needs of a new epoch are seeking expression in it." There lay a major secret of his power: he was the voice of a new era. Ministers, churches, denominations, national and world councils soon began speaking out vigorously on social questions, as they had never done before. Rauschenbusch did more after his death than he ever did in his lifetime. Details of his message might be overpassed in the swift movement of events, but the essence of his message—the social and economic transformation involved in the coming of the Kingdom of God on earth—is an integral part of the Christian gospel wherever intelligence and conscience are alive in the churches.

As Reinhold Niebuhr said of him, Rauschenbusch was "the real founder of social Christianity in this country" and "its most brilliant and generally satisfying exponent."

A Rauschenbusch Reader

PUBLISHER'S NOTE

The text of this book is set in Electra type. The introductory and explanatory material by Benson Y. Landis is set in *italic*. The writing of Walter Rauschenbusch is set in roman.

* I *

Christianity and the Social Crisis

*I*N 1907 President Theodore Roosevelt pressed his relentless campaign against "the trusts," and made himself known as a "trust-buster." Judge Kenesaw Mountain Landis, then a federal judge, fined the Standard Oil Company of Indiana $29,240,000 for accepting rebates, although on appeal the decision was reversed and the fine was not paid. In 1906 President Roosevelt had recommended an inheritance tax, in the course of a speech in Washington. He had also broken precedent and gone to the city of Panama, thus becoming the first president to pass beyond the jurisdiction of the American flag. On January 1, 1907, the Pure Food Law became effective.

In October and November of 1907 there was a severe financial panic. Wall Street spokesmen freely called it Roosevelt's panic, and tried to account for various ills and troubles by blaming the President. Elbert H. Gary invited leaders in the steel industry to a series of dinners followed by discussions which were credited by his friends with stabilizing the steel industry, but described by his opponents as attempts to create pools and agreements in violation of the antitrust laws.

Tom Johnson, mayor of Cleveland, read Henry George's writings and was converted to the single tax, after which he fought for public ownership of the city's streetcars. A rising young Socialist orator, Eugene Debs of Terre Haute, publically characterized the Supreme Court as the tool of its capitalist masters. The first all-steel Pullman cars were used by visitors to the Jamestown Exposition in Virginia, while the public pondered whether man could ever learn to fly.

Theodore Roosevelt kept hammering away at his conservation program, but announced in December, 1907, that he would not seek re-election. The same month the Atlantic Fleet of the United States Navy was sent by its Commander-in-Chief on a tour of Pacific waters and thence around the world. Some saw in this venture, following on the heels of the signing of the peace treaty of the Russo-Japanese War, a

1

further swaggering of the Big Stick. Some preachers discussed militaristic tendencies in their pulpits, but on the whole the clergy's world-mindedness was confined to foreign missions.

For most of the American public literature was still in its homey stage and the stage remained classical or melodramatic. Many were thrilled by Uncle Tom's Cabin, Ten Nights in a Bar Room, and the poetry of James Whitcomb Riley, who considered the whole state of Indiana a big country fair. It was still an America of the horse and buggy that said grace before meals; went to divine service twice on Sunday, and paid attention to Sabbath observance. Many Methodists, Baptists, and Presbyterians were much worried by Lutheran immigrants who attended church regularly but also drank beer, and by Roman Catholics who dutifully went to mass on Sunday morning and had a good time in the afternoon. Good people did not go into the divorce courts.

Young people's organizations raised money to send children from city slums into the country for two weeks in the summer, and ministers began to preach on the causes of slums. The welfare of children in cities came to the fore in public attention. The sweatshop did not appeal to many Americans, and early advocates of child-labor laws began winning a hearing. In the cities, ministers and lay people campaigned against vice and attempted to wipe out red-light districts.

Into this America came Christianity and the Social Crisis (New York, The Macmillan Company, 1907). It was, as Dr. Fosdick points out, a dangerous book. Now it is often regarded as the first of a series of major works that contributed significantly to the "moralization" and the "humanization" of theology in America. This was the conclusion, for example, of the late Bishop Francis J. McConnell of the Methodist Church. In 1941 Bishop McConnell noted that up to Rauschenbusch's time the study of theology was under the influence of those who emphasized formal deduction. Rauschenbusch broke with it with his cogent commentary on human need in relation to a reinterpretation of the teachings of Jesus.

The book was written, said the author, to discharge a debt owed by the pastor of the Second German Baptist Church "to the working people on the west side of New York City," whose life he had shared for eleven years prior to 1897. He hoped his writing would help take from them the pressures that bore them down and increase the forces that sustained them.

In the infant labor movement, Rauschenbusch saw promise and recommended that churches seek its aid in social reform. He pointed out how the rapid development of industry and the closing of the western frontier had resulted in much misery for the masses in the cities; it was they who were paying a considerable portion of the social cost of the swift economic changes. Accustomed to extremes of wealth and poverty, the people themselves had small concern that the functions of government should be expanded for social welfare. Accustomed, too, to America's geographical isolation they had only a theoretical interest in the international scene where the precarious balance of power was to be rudely disturbed by World War I. To this general frame of mind a social prophet wrote his book.

Rauschenbusch, a powerful writer, made a plea that religion play a momentous part in the social crisis that confronted the people. He determined to arouse the halting and groping conscience of Christendom. He discussed the Hebrew prophets, the social aims of Jesus, the social impetus of primitive Christianity, the handicap of a churchly Christianity that followed the primitive church. Now was the time for social evangelization. In large part, his was a biblical study. The Kingdom of God was the center of all of Jesus' teachings and love was the great society-molding force.

Since Rauschenbusch's time a powerful and pragmatic American labor movement has established itself. The functions of government have been vastly expanded, particularly in social welfare. There has been a tremendous growth of the American economy. In the international realm there has been great conflict, the rise of the techniques of mass warfare, and the search for effective means of negotiation, conciliation, and organization for keeping the peace. Hindsight discloses a measure of inevitability in these forces, but Rauschenbusch wrote when foresight cast the lines of public participation in them.

Since Rauschenbusch's era there has undoubtedly been a degree of disillusionment among many social liberals. The social gospel was adapted and adopted by religious groups not in the evangelical circle and among those with conservative bent there has been criticism of the many earlier advocates of the social gospel as humanists who believed that social progress would come by evolution. For some the emphasis swung to individualism, and it became popular to support a theology that de-emphasized human instrumentality. But the early 1950's brought signs of a revival of interest in work as a Christian vocation and dissatisfaction with a purely individualistic religion; again there was a turning of attention to a broader social context, as the prophet of Rochester advocated fifty years ago.

The selections from Christianity and the Social Crisis that follow are portions of all the chapters.

*

INTRODUCTION

WESTERN civilization is passing through a social revolution unparalleled in history for scope and power. Its coming was inevitable. The religious, political, and intellectual revolutions of the past five centuries, which together created the modern world, necessarily had to culminate in an economic and social revolution such as is now upon us.

By universal consent, this social crisis is the overshadowing problem of our generation. The industrial and commercial life of the advanced nations are in the throes of it. In politics all issues and methods are undergoing upheaval and realignment as the social movement advances. In the world of thought all the young and serious minds are absorbed in the solution of the social problems. Even literature and art point like compass needles to this magnetic pole of all our thought.

The social revolution has been slow in reaching our country. We have been exempt, not because we had solved the problems, but because we had not yet confronted them. We have now arrived, and all the characteristic conditions of American life will henceforth combine to make the social struggle here more intense than anywhere else. The vastness and the free sweep of our concentrated wealth on the one side, the independence, intelligence, moral vigor, and political power of the common people on the other side, promise a long-drawn grapple of contesting forces which may well make the heart of every American patriot sink within him.

It is realized by friend and foe that religion can play, and must play, a momentous part in this irrepressible conflict.

The Church, the organized expression of the religious life of the past, is one of the most potent institutions and forces in Western civilization. Its favor and moral influence are wooed by all parties. It cannot help throwing its immense weight on one side or the other. If it tries not to act, it thereby acts; and in any case its choice will be decisive for its own future.

Apart from the organized Church, the religious spirit is a factor of incalculable power in the making of history. In the idealistic spirits that lead and in the masses that follow, the religious spirit always intensifies thought, enlarges hope, unfetters daring, evokes the willingness to sacrifice, and gives coherence in the fight. Under the warm breath of religious faith, all social institutions become plastic. The religious spirit removes mountains and tramples on impossibilities. Unless the economic and intellectual factors are strongly reinforced by religious enthusiasm, the whole social movement may prove abortive, and the New Era may die before it comes to birth.

It follows that the relation between Christianity and the social crisis is one of the most pressing questions for all intelligent men who realize the power of religion, and most of all for the religious leaders of the people who give direction to the forces of religion.

The question has, in fact, been discussed frequently and earnestly, but it is plain to any thoughtful observer that in covering so vast a field of history and in touching on such a multitude of questions, error and incompleteness are certain, and the writer can claim only that he has tried to do honest work. Moreover, it is impossible to handle questions so vital to the economic, the social, and the moral standing of great and antagonistic classes of men, without jarring precious interests and convictions, and without giving men the choice between the bitterness of social repentance and the bitterness of moral resentment. I can frankly affirm that I have written with malice toward none and with charity for all. Even where I judge men to have done wrong, I find it easy to sympathize with them in the temptations which made the wrong almost inevitable, and in the points of view in which they entrench themselves to save their self-respect. I have tried—so far as erring human judgment permits—to lift the issues out of the plane of personal selfishness and hate, and to put them where the white light of the just and pitying spirit of Jesus can play upon them. If I have failed in that effort, it is my sin. If others in reading fail to respond in the same spirit, it is their sin. In a few years all our restless and angry hearts will be quiet in death, but those who come after us will live in the world which our sins have blighted or which our love of right has redeemed. Let us do our thinking on these great questions, not with our eyes fixed on our bank account, but with a wise outlook on the fields of the future and with the consciousness that the spirit of the Eternal is seeking to distill from our lives some essence of righteousness before they pass away.

*

THE HISTORICAL ROOTS OF CHRISTIANITY:
THE HEBREW PROPHETS

THE life and thought of the Old Testament prophets are more to us than classical illustrations and sidelights. They are an integral part of the thought life of Christianity. From the beginning the Christian

Church appropriated the Bible of Israel as its own book and thereby made the history of Israel part of the history of Christendom. That history lives in the heart of the Christian nations with a very real spiritual force. The average American knows more about David than about King Arthur, and more about the exodus from Egypt than about the emigration of the Puritans. Throughout the Christian centuries the historical material embodied in the Old Testament has been regarded as not merely instructive, but as authoritative. The social ideas drawn from it have been powerful factors in all attempts of Christianity to influence social and political life. In so far as men have attempted to use the Old Testament as a code of model laws and institutions and have applied these to modern conditions, regardless of the historical connections, these attempts have left a trail of blunder and disaster. In so far as they have caught the spirit that burned in the hearts of the prophets and breathed in gentle humanity through the Mosaic Law, the influence of the Old Testament has been one of the great permanent forces making for democracy and social justice. However our views of the Bible may change, every religious man will continue to recognize that to the elect minds of the Jewish people God gave so vivid a consciousness of the divine will that, in its main tendencies at least, their life and thought carry a permanent authority for all who wish to know the higher right of God. Their writings are like channel buoys anchored by God, and we shall do well to heed them now that the roar of an angry surf is in our ears.

We shall confine this brief study of the Old Testament to the prophets, because they are the beating heart of the Old Testament. Modern study has shown that they were the real makers of the unique religious life of Israel. If all that proceeded from them, directly or indirectly, were eliminated from the Old Testament, there would be little left to appeal to the moral and religious judgment of the modern world. Moreover, a comprehension of the essential purpose and spirit of the prophets is necessary for a comprehension of the purpose and spirit of Jesus and of genuine Christianity. In Jesus and the primitive Church the prophetic spirit rose from the dead. To the ceremonial aspects of Jewish religion Jesus was either indifferent or hostile; the thought of the prophets was the spiritual food that he assimilated in his own process of growth. With them he linked his points of view, the convictions which he regarded as axiomatic. Their spirit was to him what the soil and climate of a country are to its flora. The real meaning of his life and the real direction of his purposes can be understood only in that historical connection.

Thus a study of the prophets is not only an interesting part in the history of social movements but it is indispensable for any full comprehension of the social influence exerted by historical Christianity, and for any true comprehension of the mind of Jesus Christ.

For the purposes of this book it is not necessary to follow the work of the prophets in their historical sequence. We shall simply try to lay bare those large and permanent characteristics which are common to that remarkable series of men and which bear on the question in hand.

The fundamental conviction of the prophets, which distinguished them from the ordinary religious life of their day, was the conviction that God demands righteousness and demands nothing but righteousness.

The prophets were public men and their interest was in public affairs. Some of them were statesmen of the highest type. All of them interpreted past history, shaped present history, and foretold future history on the basis of the conviction that God rules with righteousness in the affairs of nations, and that only what is just, and not what is expedient and profitable, shall endure. Samuel was the creator of two dynasties. Nathan and Gad were the political advisers of David. Nathan determined the succession of Solomon. The seed of revolutionary aspirations against the dynasty of David was dropped into the heart of Jeroboam by the prophet Ahijah of Shiloh. Some of the prophets would get short shrift in a European state as religious demagogues. The overthrow of the dynasty of Omri in the Northern Kingdom was the result of a conspiracy between the prophetic party under Elisha and General Jehu, and resulted in a massacre so fearful that it staggered even the Oriental political conscience. On the other hand the insight of Isaiah into the international situation of his day saved his people for a long time from being embroiled in the destructive upheavals that buried other peoples, and gave it thirty years of peace amid almost universal war. The sufferings of Jeremiah came upon him chiefly because he took the unpopular side in national politics. If he and others had confined themselves to "religion," they could have said what they liked.

Our modern religious horizon and our conception of the character of a religious leader and teacher are so different that it is not easy to understand men who saw the province of religion chiefly in the broad reaches of civic affairs and international relations. Our philosophical and economic individualism has affected our religious thought so deeply that we hardly comprehend the prophetic views of an organic national life and of national sin and salvation. We usually conceive of the community as a loose sandheap of individuals and this difference in the fundamental point of view distorts the utterances of the prophets as soon as we handle them. For instance, one of our most beautiful revival

texts is the invitation: "Though your sins be as scarlet, they shall be
as white as snow; though they be red like crimson, they shall be as
wool." The words are part of the first chapter of Isaiah, to which reference has been made. The prophet throughout the chapter deals with
the national condition of the kingdom of Judah and its capital. He
describes its devastation; he ridicules the attempts to appease the national God by redoubled sacrifices; he urges instead the abolition of
social oppression and injustice as the only way of regaining God's favor
for the nation. If they would vindicate the cause of the helpless and
oppressed, then he would freely pardon; then their scarlet and crimson
guilt would be washed away. The familiar text is followed by the very
material promise of economic prosperity, and the threat of continued
war: "If ye be willing and obedient, ye shall eat the good of the land;
but if ye refuse and rebel, ye shall be devoured with the sword." Of
course the text is nobly true when it is made to express God's willingness to pardon the repentant individual, but that was not the thought
in the mind of the writer. He offered a new start to his nation on condition that it righted social wrongs. We offer free pardon to individuals
and rarely mention social wrongs.

The prophets demanded right moral conduct as the sole test and
fruit of religion, and that the morality which they had in mind was not
the private morality of detached pious souls but the social morality of
the nation. This they preached, and they backed their preaching by
active participation in public action and discussion.

The Hebrew prophets shared the fate of all leaders who are far ahead
of their times. They did not themselves achieve the triumph of their
ideas. It was achieved for them by men who did not share their spirit,
and who insensibly debased their ideals in realizing them. The ethical
monotheism of the prophets did not become common property in Judah
till the priests and scribes enforced it. That is part of the Divine Com-
edy of history. The Tories carry out the Liberal programmes. The ideas
preached by Socialists and Single Taxers are adopted by Populists, radical Democrats, and conservative Republicans successively, and in coming years the great parties will take credit for championing ideas which
they did their best to stifle and then to betray. It is a beneficent scheme
by which the joy of life is evened up. The "practical men" and con-
servatives have the pleasure of feeling that they are the only ones who
can really make reforms work. The prophetic minds have the satisfaction of knowing that the world must come their way whether it will
or not, because they are on the way to justice, and justice is on the way
to God.

Here then we have a succession of men perhaps unique in religious history for their moral heroism and spiritual insight. They were the moving spirits in the religious progress of their nation; the creators, directly or indirectly, of its law, its historical and poetical literature, and its piety; the men to whose personality and teaching Jesus felt most kinship; the men who still kindle modern religious enthusiasm. Most of us believe that their insight was divinely given and that the course they steered was set for them by the Captain of history.

These men were almost indifferent, if not contemptuous, about the ceremonial side of customary religion, but turned with passionate enthusiasm to moral righteousness as the true domain of religion. Where would their interest lie if they lived today?

Their religious concern was not restricted to private religion and morality, but dealt pre-eminently with the social and political life of their nation. Would they limit its range today?

Their sympathy was wholly and passionately with the poor and oppressed. If they lived today, would they place the chief blame for poverty on the poor and give their admiration to the strong?

They gradually rose above the kindred prophets of other nations through their moral interest in national affairs, and that their spiritual progress and education were intimately connected with their open-eyed comprehension of the larger questions of contemporary history. Is it likely that the same attitude of mind which enlarged and purified the religion of the Hebrew leaders would deteriorate and endanger the religion of Christian leaders?

We have seen that the religious concern in politics ceased only when politics ceased; that religious individualism was a triumph of faith under abnormal conditions and not a normal type of religious life; and that the enforced withdrawal of religion from the wider life was one cause for the later narrowness of Judaism. Does this warrant the assumption that religion is most normal when it is most the affair of the individual?

The sane political programme and the wise historical insight of the great prophets turned into apocalyptic dreams and bookish calculations when the nation lost its political self-government and training. How wise is it for the Christian leaders of a democratic nation to take their interpretation of God's purposes in history and their theories about the coming of the Kingdom of God from the feeblest and most decadent age of Hebrew thought?

The true prophets opposed the complacent optimism of the people and of their popular spokesmen, and gave warning of disaster as long as it was coming. If they lived among the resent symptoms of social and moral decay, would they sing a lullaby or sound the reveille?

No true prophet will copy a prophet. Their garb, their mannerisms of language, the vehemence of their style, belong to their age and not to ours. But if we believe in their divine mission and in the divine origin of the religion in which they were the chief factors, we cannot repudiate what was fundamental in their lives. If anyone holds that religion is essentially ritual and sacramental; or that it is purely personal; or that God is on the side of the rich; or that social interest is likely to lead preachers astray; he must prove his case with his eye on the Hebrew prophets, and the burden of proof is with him.

*

THE SOCIAL AIMS OF JESUS

THE historical background which we have just sketched must ever be kept in mind in understanding the life and purpose of Jesus. He was not merely an initiator, but a consummator. Like all great minds that do not merely imagine Utopias, but actually advance humanity to a new epoch, he took the situation and material furnished to him by the past and molded that into a fuller approximation to the divine conception within him. He embodied the prophetic stream of faith and hope. He linked his work to that of John the Baptist as the one contemporary fact to which he felt most inward affinity.

Jesus began his preaching with the call: "The time is fulfilled; the kingdom of God is now close at hand; repent and believe in the glad news." [1] The Kingdom of God continued to be the center of all his teaching as recorded by the synoptic gospels. His parables, his moral instructions, and his prophetic predictions all bear on that.

We have no definition of what he meant by the phrase. His audience needed no definition. It was then a familiar conception and phrase. The new thing was simply that this kingdom was at last on the point of coming.

We are not at all in that situation today. Anyone who has tried to grasp the idea will have realized how vague and elusive it seems. It stands today for quite a catalogue of ideas. To the ordinary reader of the Bible, "inheriting the kingdom of heaven" simply means being saved and going to heaven. For others it means the millennium. For some the organized Church; for others "the invisible Church." For the mystic it means the hidden life with God. The truth is that the idea in

[1] Mark 1:15.

the sense in which Jesus and his audiences understood it almost completely passed out of Christian thought as soon as Christianity passed from the Jewish people and found its spiritual home within the great Graeco-Roman world. The historical basis for the idea was wanting there. The phrase was taken along, just as an emigrant will carry a water jar with him; but the water from the well of Bethlehem evaporated and it was now used to dip water from the wells of Ephesus or from the Nile and Tiber. The Greek world cherished no such national religious hope as the prophets had ingrained in Jewish thought; on the other hand it was intensely interested in the future life for the individual, and in the ascetic triumph over flesh and matter. Thus the idea which had been the center of Christ's thought was not at all the center of the Church's thought, and even the comprehension of his meaning was lost and overlaid. Only some remnants of it persisted in the millennial hope and in the organic conception of the Church.

The historical study of our own day has made the first thorough attempt to understand this fundamental thought of Jesus in the sense in which he used it, but the results of this investigation are not at all completed. There are a hundred critical difficulties in the way of a sure and consistent interpretation that would be acceptable to all investigators. The limits of space and the purpose of this book will not permit me to do justice to the conflicting views. I shall have to set down my own results with only an occasional reference to the difficulties that beset them.

When Jesus used the phrase "the Kingdom of God," it inevitably evoked that whole sphere of thought in the minds of his hearers. If he did not mean by it the substance of what they meant by it, it was a mistake to use the term. If he did not mean the consummation of the theocratic hope, but merely an internal blessedness for individuals with the hope of getting to heaven, why did he use the words around which all the collective hopes clustered? In that case it was not only a misleading but a dangerous phrase. It unfettered the political hopes of the crowd; it drew down on him the suspicion of the government; it actually led to his death.

Unless we have clear proof to the contrary, we must assume that in the main the words meant the same thing to him and to his audiences. But it is very possible that he seriously modified and corrected the popular conception. That is in fact the process with every great, creative religious mind: the connection with the past is maintained and the old terms are used, but they are set in new connections and filled with new qualities. In the teaching of Jesus we find that he consciously opposed some features of the popular hope and sought to make it truer.

For one thing he would have nothing to do with bloodshed and violence. When the crowds that were on their way to the Passover gathered around him in the solitude on the Eastern shore of the lake and wanted to make him king and march on the capital, he eluded them by sending his inflammable disciples away in the boat, and himself going up among the rocks to pray till the darkness dispersed the crowd.[2] Alliance with the Messianic force-revolution was one of the temptations which he confronted at the outset and repudiated;[3] he would not set up God's Kingdom by using the devil's means of hatred and blood. With the glorious idealism of faith and love Jesus threw away the sword and advanced on the entrenchments of wrong with hand outstretched and heart exposed.

There was a revolutionary consciousness in Jesus; not, of course, in the common use of the word "revolutionary," which connects it with violence and bloodshed. But Jesus knew that he had come to kindle a fire on earth. Much as he loved peace, he knew that the actual result of his work would be not peace but the sword. His mother in her song had recognized in her own experience the settled custom of God to "put down the proud and exalt them of low degree," to "fill the hungry with good things and to send the rich empty away."[4] King Robert of Sicily recognized the revolutionary ring in those phrases, and thought it well that the Magnificat was sung only in Latin. The son of Mary expected a great reversal of values. The first would be last and the last would be first.[5] He saw that what was exalted among man was an abomination before God,[6] and therefore these exalted things had no glamour for his eye. This revolutionary note runs even through the Beatitudes where we should least expect it. The point of them is that henceforth those were to be blessed whom the world had not blessed, for the Kingdom of God would reverse their relative standing. Now the poor and the hungry and sad were to be satisfied and comforted; the meek who had been shouldered aside by the ruthless would get their chance to inherit the earth, and conflict and persecution would be inevitable in the process.[7]

We are apt to forget that his attack on the religious leaders and authorities of his day was of revolutionary boldness and thoroughness. He called the ecclesiastical leaders hypocrites, blind leaders who fumbled in their casuistry, and everywhere missed the decisive facts in teach-

[2] Matt. 14:22–23.
[3] Matt. 4:8–10.
[4] Luke 1:52–53.

[5] Mark 10:31.
[6] Luke 16:15.
[7] Matt. 5:1–12.

ing right and wrong. Their piety was no piety; their law was inadequate; they harmed the men whom they wanted to convert.[8] Even the publicans and harlots had a truer piety than theirs.[9] If we remember that religion was still the foundation of the Jewish state, and that the religious authorities were the pillars of existing society, much as in medieval Catholic Europe, we shall realize how revolutionary were his invectives. It was like Luther anathematizing the Catholic hierarchy.

Jesus was not a child of this world. He did not revere the men it called great; he did not accept its customs and social usages as final; his moral conceptions did not run along the grooves marked out by it. He nourished within his soul the ideal of a common life so radically different from the present that it involved a reversal of values, a revolutionary displacement of existing relations. This ideal was not merely a beautiful dream to solace his soul. He lived it out in his own daily life. He urged others to live that way. He held that it was the only true life, and that the ordinary way was misery and folly. He dared to believe that it would triumph. When he saw that the people were turning from him, and that his nation had chosen the evil way and was drifting toward the rocks that would destroy it, unutterable sadness filled his soul, but he never abandoned his faith in the final triumph of that Kingdom of God for which he had lived. For the present, the cross; but beyond the cross, the Kingdom of God. If he was not to achieve it now, he would return and do it then.

That was the faith of Jesus. Have his followers shared it? We shall see later what changes and limitations the original purpose and spirit of Christianity suffered in the course of history. But the Church has never been able to get entirely away from the revolutionary spirit of Jesus. It is an essential doctrine of Christianity that the world is fundamentally good and practically bad, for it was made by God, but is now controlled by sin. If a man wants to be a Christian, he must stand over against things as they are and condemn them in the name of that higher conception of life which Jesus revealed. If a man is satisfied with things as they are, he belongs to the other side. For many centuries the Church felt so deeply that the Christian conception of life and the actual social life are incompatible, that anyone who wanted to live the genuine Christian life, had to leave the world and live in a monastic community. Protestantism has abandoned the monastic life and settled down to live in the world. If that implies that it accepts the present condition as good and final, it means a silencing of its Christian protest

[8] See the whole of Matt. 23.
[9] Matt. 21:23–32.

and its surrender to "the world." There is another alternative. Ascetic Christianity called the world evil and left it. Humanity is waiting for a ✗ revolutionary Christianity which will call the world evil and change it. We do not want "to blow all our existing institutions to atoms," but we do want to remold every one of them. A tank of gasolene can blow a car sky-high in a single explosion, or push it to the top of a hill in a perpetual succession of little explosions. We need a combination between the faith of Jesus in the need and the possibility of the Kingdom of God, and the modern comprehension of the organic development of human society.

Jesus was not a mere social reformer. Religion was the heart of his life, and all that he said on social relations was said from the religious point of view. He has been called the first socialist. He was more; he was the first real man, the inaugurator of a new humanity. But as such he bore within him the germs of a new social and political order. He was too great to be the Saviour of a fractional part of human life. His redemption extends to all human needs and powers and relations. Theologians have felt no hesitation in founding a system of speculative thought on the teachings of Jesus, and yet Jesus was never an inhabitant of the realm of speculative thought. He has been made the founder and organizer of a great ecclesiastical machine, which derives authority for its offices and institutions from him, and yet "hardly any problem of exegesis is more difficult than to discover in the gospels an administrative or organizing or ecclesiastical Christ." [10] There is at least as much justification in invoking his name today as the champion of a great movement for a more righteous social life. He was neither a theologian, nor an ecclesiastic, nor a socialist. But if we were forced to classify him either with the great theologians who elaborated the fine distinctions of scholasticism; or with the mighty popes and princes of the Church who built up their power in his name; or with the men who are giving their heart and life to the propaganda of a new social system—where should we place him?

*

THE SOCIAL IMPETUS OF PRIMITIVE CHRISTIANITY

IN SPITE of the defectiveness and one-sidedness of the historical sources furnishing the material for our study, we have found an abundant and throbbing social life in primitive Christianity.

[10] Peabody, *Jesus Christ and the Social Question*, 89.

All of its theories involved a bold condemnation of existing society. Whether that society was to be overthrown by a divine catastrophe of judgment or displaced and absorbed in the higher life of the Christian community, in any case it was to go. The future of society belonged to that new life originated by Christ. Christianity was conscious of a far-reaching and thorough political and social mission. This is the more remarkable because it was weak in numbers, apparently withdrawn from the larger life of society, and without any present or any apparent future influence on the organized life of the civilized world. Such convictions, cherished in the face of such odds, argue that it was launched with a powerful and invincible social impetus, and that the consciousness of a regenerating mission for social life is inseparable from the highest form of religion.

The strength of its social tendencies was not exhausted by its hopes for the future. It immediately began to build a society within which the new ideals of moral and social life were to be realized at once, so far as the limitations of an evil environment permitted. The primitive Christian churches were not ecclesiastical organizations so much as fraternal communities. They withdrew their members from the social life outside and organized a complete social life within their circle. Their common meals expressed and created social solidarity. Their organization at first was executive and was devised to meet social and moral, rather than religious and doctrinal, needs. Their income was completely devoted to fraternal help. As organizations for mutual help and fraternal co-operation the Christian churches became indispensable to the city population and invincible by the government.

This fraternal helpfulness was more than mere religious kindliness. It was animated by the consciousness of a creative social mission and accompanied by a spirit of social unrest which proves the existence of powerful currents of democratic feeling. Under the first impact of its ideas and spirit, men and women tried to realize at once those social changes which have actually been accomplished in centuries of development. This impulse proves that a reconstructive social dynamic inheres in Christianity and must find an outlet in some form, slow or swift.

We were prepared to find a long drop downward when we passed from Jesus to the thoughts and doings of his followers. We did find it so. In their religious life not even the greatest maintained his level, and the lowest groped in a density of superstition and puerrile legalism which makes it seem queer to put the great name of Jesus upon them. And yet the higher impulse was implanted. Give it time! Humanity is an organism that passes through a long series of metamorphoses, and it measures its seasons by centuries. The purification of the religious life, the comprehension of the real meaning and spirit of Christ, have made marvelous progress in recent times.

In the social direction of the religious spirit we found a like decline. There is not the same unerring penetration of judgment on social morality, not the same eagle-eyed boldness of hope and faith for the future, not the same sweet reasonableness about the slow methods of realizing the ultimate goal, not the same lovable love nor the same power to heal and save the broken and diseased members of the social body. There is a good deal of crude thinking, of sectarian narrowness and pride, of ecclesiastical ambition, of complete forgetfulness of the high mission to the world. And yet there is the germ of a new social life for humanity, the conception of a social morality based on love and world-wide in its obligation. Give it time! This, too, under ever-changing forms, may work its way, and triumph yet. The modern emancipation of the intellectual life began in the Renaissance of the fifteenth century and is not finished yet. The modern emancipation of the religious life began in the Reformation of the sixteenth century and is not finished yet. The modern emancipation of the political life began in the Puritan Revolution of the seventeenth century and is not finished yet. The modern emancipation of the industrial life began in the nineteenth century and is not finished yet. Let us have patience. Let us have hope. And above all let us have faith.

※

WHY HAS CHRISTIANITY NEVER UNDERTAKEN THE WORK OF SOCIAL RECONSTRUCTION?

HERE, then, is a vast force which by all the tradition of its origin and by its very essence is committed to the moral reconstruction of human society. It has had time and opportunity. Why, then, has it not reconstituted the social life of Christendom?

Two answers may be given to this question, each the opposite of the other.

It may be replied that in spite of the spread and power of the Church any actual reconstruction was impossible. Christianity was rising when the ancient world was breaking down. By the time the Church had gained sufficient power to exercise a controlling influence, the process of social decay, like the breakdown of a physical organism in a wasting disease, was beyond remedy. The unsolved social questions of pagan centuries had created a despotic government, a venal and rapacious bureaucracy, a vicious and parasitic aristocracy of wealth, and a vast mass of nerveless and hopeless hereditary paupers. The impact of the Teutonic barbarians merely crumpled up an organization that was hollow within. What power could save a State that was rotten to the core?

Others again will return the opposite reply. If we ask why Christianity has not reconstituted society, they will say it has done so. Has it not lifted woman to equality and companionship with man, secured the sanctity and stability of marriage, changed parental despotism to parental service, and eliminated unnatural vice, the abandonment of children, blood revenge, and the robbery of the shipwrecked from the customs of Christian nations? Has it not abolished slavery, mitigated war, covered all lands with a network of charities to uplift the poor and the fallen, fostered the institutions of education, aided the progress of civil liberty and social justice, and diffused a softening tenderness throughout human life?

Rauschenbusch elaborated both these positions. He remarked that those who thought the influence of the Church had been great were always "tempted" to contrast the darkest aspects of pagan society with the brightest aspects of societies in which the Christian church had functioned. "In the next place, the social effects which are usually enumerated do not constitute a reconstruction of society on a Christian basis, but were mainly a suppression of some of the most glaring evils in the social system of the time. . . . In the third place, the most important effects of Christianity went out from it without the intention of the Church, or even against its will. . . . The Church has often been indifferent or hostile to the effects which it had itself produced."

Rauschenbusch found more convincing the evidence that Christianity had never undertaken the work of social reconstruction. "The apostles undertook no social propaganda. . . . Paul and the entire primitive church . . . expected the very speedy coming of the Lord. . . . The hope of the Lord's coming necessarily involved the hope that the empire and its social life would come to an end. . . . How could a social life so fundamentally wrong be reconstructed? . . . The otherworldliness of early Christianity was only one aspect of its general ascetic view of life. . . . In ever-widening circles the monastic ideal laid hold of men." Again, "when Christianity turned its deepest interest from ethical conduct to sacramental ritual, it thereby paralyzed its power of moral transformation."

"A parallel fact is the deflecting influence of dogma." Further developments were the emergence of a tight ecclesiastical organization, and of "the churchliness of Christianity." "The influence of the church *in humane legislation was neutralized by her anxiety to secure benefits for herself . . . The Church as a body has been dependent on the state and therefore subservient to it." The democracy of the Church disappeared. There was a "lack of scientific comprehension of social development." The Reformation brought on a "slow turn" of events so that the intellectual prerequisites for social reconstruction, formerly lacking, were "now at hand."*

To a religious man the contemplation of the larger movements of history brings a profound sense of God's presence and overruling power. "Behind the dim unknown standeth God within the shadow, keeping watch above his own." [1] Christ is immanent in humanity and is slowly disciplining the nations and lifting them to share in his spirit. By great processes of self-purification the alien infusions in Christianity have been eliminated, and Christianity itself is being converted to Christ.

But all these larger movements, by which the essential genius of Christianity is being set free, have also equipped it for a conscious regenerating influence on the common life of the race. It is now fitter for its social mission than ever before.

At the same time when Christianity has thus attained to its adolescence and moral maturity, there is a piercing call from the world about it, summoning all moral strength and religious heroism to save the Christian world from social strangulation and death. That call will be the subject of the next chapter. The converging of these two lines of development is providential. We are standing at the turning of the ways. We are actors in a great historical drama. It rests upon us to decide if a new era is to dawn in the transformation of the world into the kingdom of God, or if Western civilization is to descend to the graveyard of dead civilizations and God will have to try once more.

*

THE PRESENT CRISIS

NEXT came a discussion of the industrial revolution and its social effects—"social misery" for large numbers of people. References were made to concentrations of the holding of land and other wealth, the drive for profits, the insecurity of the workers in industry, the existence of large groups of people "without property," prevailing inequality, the

[1] James Russell Lowell, "The Present Crisis."

strains under which political democracy labored, "the undermining of the family."

*

I N the last resort the only hope is in the moral forces which can be summoned to the rescue. If there are statesmen, products, and apostles who set truth and justice above selfish advancement; if their call finds a response in the great body of the people; if a new tide of religious faith and moral enthusiasm creates new standards of duty and a new capacity for self-sacrifice; if the strong learn to direct their love of power to the uplifting of the people and see the highest self-assertion in self-sacrifice—then the entrenchments of vested wrong will melt away; the stifled energy of the people will leap forward; the atrophied members of the social body will be filled with a fresh flow of blood; and a regenerate nation will look with the eyes of youth across the fields of the future.

The cry of "Crisis! Crisis!" has become a weariness. Every age and every year are critical and fraught with destiny. Yet in the widest survey of history Western civilization is now at a decisive point in its development.

Will some Gibbon of Mongol race sit by the shore of the Pacific in A.D. 3000 and write on the "Decline and Fall of the Christian Empire"? If so, he will probably describe the nineteenth and twentieth centuries as the golden age when outwardly life flourished as never before, but when that decay, which resulted in the gradual collapse of the twenty-first and twenty-second centuries, was already far advanced.

Or will the twentieth century mark for the future historian the real adolescence of humanity, the great emancipation from barbarism and from the paralysis of injustice, and the beginning of a progress in the intellectual, social, and moral life of mankind to which all past history has no parallel?

It will depend almost wholly on the moral forces which the Christian nations can bring to the fighting line against wrong, and the fighting energy of those moral forces will again depend on the degree to which they are inspired by religious faith and enthusiasm. It is either a revival of social religion or the deluge.

*

THE STAKE OF THE CHURCH IN THE SOCIAL MOVEMENT

THE demoralization of society ought to appeal most powerfully to the Church, for the Church is to be the incarnation of the Christ-spirit on earth, the organized conscience of Christendom. It should be swiftest to awaken to every undeserved suffering, bravest to speak against every wrong, and strongest to rally the moral forces of the community against everything that threatens the better life among men.

The gospel, to have full power over an age, must be the highest expression of the moral and religious truths held by that age. If it lags behind and deals in outgrown conceptions of life and duty, it will lose power over the ablest minds and the young men first, and gradually over all. In our thought today the social problems irresistibly take the lead. If the Church has no live and bold thought on this dominant question of modern life, its teaching authority on all other questions will dwindle and be despised. It cannot afford to have young men sniff the air as in a stuffy room when they enter the sphere of religious thought. When the world is in travail with a higher ideal of justice, the Church dare not ignore it if it would retain its moral leadership. On the other hand, if the Church does incorporate the new social terms in its synthesis of truth, they are certain to throw new light on all the older elements of its teaching. The conception of race sin and race salvation become comprehensible once more to those who have made the idea of social solidarity in good and evil a part of their thought. The law of sacrifice loses its arbitrary and mechanical aspect when we understand the vital union of all humanity. Individualistic Christianity has almost lost sight of the great idea of the Kingdom of God, which was the inspiration and center of the thought of Jesus. Social Christianity would once more enable us to understand the purpose and thought of Jesus and take the veil from our eyes when we read the synoptic gospels.

The social crisis offers a great opportunity for the infusion of new life and power into the religious thought of the church. It also offers the chance for progress in its life. When the broader social outlook widens the purpose of a Christian man beyond the increase of his church, he lifts up his eyes and sees that there are others who are at work for humanity besides his denomination. Common work for social welfare is the best common ground for the various religious bodies and the best training school for practical Christian unity. The strong movement for Christian union in our country has been largely prompted by the realization of social needs, and is led by men who have felt the attraction of the Kingdom of God as something greater than any denomination and as the common object of all. Thus the divisions which were caused in the past by differences in dogma and church polity may perhaps be healed by unity of interest in social salvation.

As we have seen, the industrial and commercial life today is dominated by principles antagonistic to the fundamental principles of Christianity, and it is so difficult to live a Christian life in the midst of it that few men even try. If production could be organized on a basis of co-operative fraternity; if distribution could at least approximately be determined by justice; if all men could be conscious that their labor contributed to the welfare of all and that their personal well-being was dependent on the prosperity of the Commonwealth; if predatory business and parasitic wealth ceased and all men lived only by their labor; if the luxury of unearned wealth no longer made us all feverish with covetousness and a simpler life became the fashion; if our time and strength were not used up either in getting a bare living or in amassing unusable wealth and we had more leisure for the higher pursuits of the mind and the soul—then there might be a chance to live such a life of gentleness and brotherly kindness and tranquillity of heart as Jesus desired for men. It may be that the co-operative Commonwealth would give us the first chance in history to live a really Christian life without retiring from the world, and would make the Sermon on the Mount a philosophy of life feasible for all who care to try.

This is the stake of the Church in the social crisis. If society continues to disintegrate and decay, the Church will be carried down with it. If the Church can rally such moral forces that injustice will be overcome and fresh red blood will course in a sounder social organism, it will itself rise to higher liberty and life. Doing the will of God it will have new visions of God. With a new message will come a new authority. If the salt lose its saltness, it will be trodden under foot. If the Church fulfills its prophetic functions, it may bear the prophet's reproach for a time, but it will have the prophet's vindication thereafter.

The conviction has always been embedded in the heart of the Church that "the world"—society as it is—is evil and some time is to make way for a true human society in which the spirit of Jesus Christ shall rule. For fifteen hundred years those who desired to live a truly Christian life withdrew from the evil world to live a life apart. But the principle of such an ascetic departure from the world is dead in modern life. There are only two other possibilities. The Church must either condemn the world and seek to change it, or tolerate the world and conform to it. In the latter case it surrenders its holiness and its mission. The other possibility has never yet been tried with full faith on a large scale. All the leadings of God in contemporary history and all the promptings of Christ's spirit in our hearts urge us to make the trial. On this choice is staked the future of the Church.

*

WHAT TO DO

I NOW suggest in what ways the moral forces latent in Christian society could be mobilized for the progressive regeneration of social life, and in what directions chiefly these forces should be exerted.

Some lines of effort frequently attempted in the past by Christian men and organizations are useless and misleading. It is fruitless to attempt to turn modern society back to conditions prevailing before power machinery and trusts had revolutionized it; or to copy biblical institutions adapted to wholly different social conditions; or to postpone the Christianizing of society to the millennium; or to found Christian communistic colonies within the competitive world; or to make the organized Church the center and manager of an improved social machinery. The force of religion can best be applied to social renewal by sending its spiritual power along the existing and natural relations of men to direct them to truer ends and govern them by higher motives.

The fundamental contribution of every man is the change of his own personality. We must repent of the sins of existing society, cast off the spell of the lies protecting our social wrongs, have faith in a higher social order, and realize in ourselves a new type of Christian manhood which seeks to overcome the evil in the present world, not by withdrawing from the world, but by revolutionizing it.

If this new type of religious character multiplies among the young men and women, they will change the world when they come to hold the controlling positions of society in their maturer years. They will give a new force to righteous and enlightened public opinion, and will apply the religious sense of duty and service to the common daily life with a new motive and directness.

The ministry, in particular, must apply the teaching functions of the pulpit to the pressing questions of public morality. It must collectively learn not to speak without adequate information; not to charge individuals with guilt in which all society shares; not to be partial, and yet to be on the side of the lost; not to yield to political partisanship, but to deal with moral questions before they become political issues and with those questions of public welfare which never do become political issues. They must lift the social questions to a religious level by faith and spiritual insight. The larger the number of ministers who attempt these untrodden ways, the safer and saner will those be who follow. By interpreting one social class to the other, they can create a disposition to make concessions and help in securing a peaceful settlement of social issues.

The force of the religious spirit should be bent toward asserting the supremacy of life over property. Property exists to maintain and develop life. It is unchristian to regard human life as a mere instrument for the production of wealth.

The religious sentiment can protect good customs and institutions against the inroads of ruthless greed, and extend their scope. It can create humane customs which the law is impotent to create. It can create the convictions and customs which are later embodied in good legislation.

Our complex society rests largely on the stewardship of delegated powers. The opportunities to profit by the betrayal of trust increase with the wealth and complexity of civilization. The most fundamental evils in past history and present conditions were due to converting stewardship into ownership. The keener moral insight created by Christianity should lend its help in scrutinizing all claims to property and power in order to detect latent public rights and to recall the recreant stewards to their duty.

Primitive society was communistic. The most valuable institutions in modern life—the family, the school, and church—are communistic. The state, too, is essentially communistic and is becoming increasingly so. During the larger part of its history the Christian Church regarded communism as the only ideal life. Christianity certainly has more affinity for co-operative and fraternal institutions than for competitive disunion. It should therefore strengthen the existing communistic institutions and aid the evolution of society from the present temporary stage of individualism to a higher form of communism.

The splendid ideal of a fraternal organization of society cannot be realized by idealists only. It must be supported by the self-interest of a powerful class. The working class, which is now engaged in its upward movement, is struggling to secure better conditions of life, an assured status for its class organizations, and ultimately the ownership of the means of production. Its success in the last great aim would mean the closing of the gap which now divides industrial society and the establishment of industry on the principle of solidarity and the method of co-operation. Christianity should enter into a working alliance with this rising class, and by its mediation secure the victory of these principles by a gradual equalization of social opportunity and power.

The first apostolate of Christianity was born from a deep fellow-feeling for social misery and from the consciousness of a great historical opportunity. Jesus saw the peasantry of Galilee following him about with their poverty and their diseases, like shepherdless sheep that have been scattered and harried by beasts of prey, and his heart had compassion on them. He felt that the harvest was ripe, but there were few to reap it. Past history had come to its culmination, but there were few who understood the situation and were prepared to cope with it. He bade his disciples to pray for laborers for the harvest, and then made them answer their own prayers by sending them out two by two to proclaim the Kingdom of God. That was the beginning of the world-wide mission of Christianity.[1]

The situation is repeated on a vaster scale today. If Jesus stood today amid our modern life, with that outlook on the condition of all humanity which observation and travel and the press would spread before him, and with the same heart of divine humanity beating in him, he would create a new apostolate to meet the new needs in a new harvest time of history.

To anyone who knows the sluggishness of humanity to good, the impregnable intrenchments of vested wrongs and the long reaches of time needed from one milestone of progress to the next, the task of setting up a Christian social order in this modern world of ours seems like a fair and futile dream. Yet in fact it is not one tithe as hopeless as when Jesus set out to do it. When he told his disciples, "Ye are the salt of the earth; ye are the light of the world," he expressed the consciousness of a great historic mission to the whole of humanity. Yet it was a Nazarene carpenter speaking to a group of Galilean peasants and fishermen. Under the circumstances at that time it was an utterance of the most daring faith—faith in himself, faith in them, faith in what he was putting into them, faith in faith. Jesus failed and was crucified, first his body by his enemies, and then his spirit by his friends; but that failure was so amazing a success that today it takes an effort on our part to realize that it required any faith on his part to inaugurate the Kingdom of God and to send out his apostolate.

[1] See Matt. 9:32–10:42.

Today, as Jesus looks out upon humanity, his spirit must leap to see the souls responsive to his call. They are sown broadcast through humanity, legions of them. The harvest field is no longer deserted. All about us we hear the clang of the whetstone and the rush of the blades through the grain and the shout of the reapers. With all our faults and our slothfulness we modern men in many ways are more on a level with the real mind of Jesus than any generation that has gone before. If that first apostolate was able to remove mountains by the power of faith, such an apostolate as Christ could now summon might change the face of the earth.

The apostolate of a new age must do the work of the sower. When the sower goes forth to sow his seed, he goes with the certainty of partial failure and the knowledge that a long time of patience and of hazard will intervene before he can hope to see the result of his work and his venture. In sowing the truth a man may never see or trace the results. The more ideal his conceptions are, and the farther they move ahead of his time, the larger will be the percentage of apparent failure. But he can afford to wait. The powers of life are on his side. He is like a man who has scattered his seed and then goes off to sleep by night and work by day, and all the while the seed, by the inscrutable chemistry of life, lays hold of the ingredients of its environment and builds them up to its own growth. The mustard seed becomes a tree. The leaven assimilates the meal by biological processes. The new life penetrates the old humanity and transforms it. Robert Owen was a sower. His co-operative communities failed. He was able to help only a small fraction of the workingmen of his day. But his moral enthusiasm and his ideas fertilized the finest and most self-sacrificing minds among the working classes. They cherished his ultimate hopes in private and worked for realizable ends in public. The Chartist movement was filled with his spirit. The most influential leaders of English unionism in its great period after the middle of the nineteenth century were Owenites. The Rochdale Pioneers were under his influence, and the great co-operative movement in England, an economic force of the first importance, grew in some measure out of the seed which Owen had scattered. Other men may own the present. The future belongs to the sower— provided he scatters seed and does not mistake the chaff for it which once was so essential to the seed and now is dead and useless.

It is inevitable that those who stand against conditions in which most men believe and by which the strongest profit, shall suffer for their stand. The little group of early Christian socialists in England, led by Maurice, Kingsley, and Hughes, now stand by common consent in the history of that generation as one of its finest products, but at that time they were bitterly assailed and misunderstood. Pastor Rudolf Todt, the first man in Germany who undertook to prove that the New Testament and the ethics of socialism have a close affinity, was almost unanimously attacked by the Church of Germany. But Jesus told his apostles at the outset that opposition would be part of their day's work. Christ equipped his Church with no legal rights to protect her; the only political right he gave his disciples was the right of being persecuted.[2] It is part of the doctrine of vicarious atonement, which is fundamental in Christianity, that the prophetic souls must vindicate by their sufferings the truth of the truth they preach.

> Disappointment's dry and bitter root,
> Envy's harsh berries, and the choking pool
> Of the world's scorn, are the right mother-milk
> To the tough hearts that pioneer their kind
> And break a pathway to those unknown realms
> That in the earth's broad shadow lie enthralled;
> Endurance is the crowning quality,
> And patience all the passion of great hearts;
> These are their stay, and when the leaden world
> Sets its hard face against their fateful thought,
> And brute strength, like a scornful conqueror,
> Clangs his huge mace down in the other scale,
> The inspired soul but flings his patience in,
> And slowly that outweighs the ponderous globe,—
> One faith against a whole earth's unbelief,
> One soul against the flesh of all mankind.[3]

The championship of social justice is almost the only way left open to a Christian nowadays to gain the crown of martyrdom. Theological heretics are rarely persecuted now. The only rival of God is Mammon, and it is only when his sacred name is blasphemed that men throw the Christians to the lions.

Even for the social heretics there is a generous readiness to listen which was unknown in the past. In our country that openness of mind is a product of our free intellectual life, our ingrained democracy, the denominational manifoldness of our religious life, and the spread of the Christian spirit. It has become an accepted doctrine among us that all great movements have obscure beginnings, and that belief tends to make men respectful toward anything that comes from some despised Nazareth. Unless a man forfeits respect by bitterness or lack of tact, he is accorded a large degree of tolerance, though he will always be

[2] Nathusius, *Mitarbeit der Kirche*, 476.
[3] James Russell Lowell, "Columbus."

made to feel the difference between himself and those who say the things that please the great.

The certainty of opposition constitutes a special call to the strong. The ministry seems to have little attraction for the sons of rich men. It is not strange when one considers the enervating trials that beset a rich man in a pastorate. But here is a mission that ought to appeal to the rich young man if he has heroic stuff in him. His assured social standing would give him an influence with rich and poor alike which others attain but slowly if at all. The fear of being blacklisted for championing justice and mercy need have no terrors for him. To use his property as a coat of mail in fighting the battles of the weak would be the best way of obeying Christ's command to the rich young ruler to sell all and give it to the poor. When Mr. Roosevelt was still Police Commissioner in New York, he said to the young men of New York: "I would teach the young men that he who has not wealth owes his first duty to his family, but he who has means owes his to the State. It is ignoble to go on heaping up money. I would preach the doctrine of work to all, and to the men of wealth the doctrine of unremunerative work." [4] The most "unremunerative work" is the work that draws opposition and animosity.

Mr. Roosevelt implies here that a man's duty to his family is the first and dominant duty, and that this exempts him in some measure from service to the larger public. It follows that the childless have a call to the dangerous work of the Kingdom of God. A man and woman who are feeding and training young citizens are performing so immense and absorbing a service to the future that they might well be exempt from taxes to the state and from sacrificial service to the Kingdom of God. If nevertheless so many of them assume these duties in addition, the childless man and woman will have to do heroic work in the trenches before they can rank on the same level. It is not fair to ask a man with children to give his time and strength as freely to public causes as if he had none. It is still more unfair to expect him to risk the bread and the prospects of his family in championing dangerous causes as freely as if he risked only himself. The childless people should adopt the whole coming generation of children and fight to make the world more habitable for them as for their own brood. The unmarried and the childless should enlist in the new apostolate and march on the forlorn hopes with Jesus Christ.

In asking for faith in the possibility of a new social order, we ask for no Utopian delusion. We know well that there is no perfection for

[4] Jacob A. Riis, *Theodore Roosevelt, the Citizen.*

man in this life: there is only growth toward perfection. In personal religion we look with seasoned suspicion at any one who claims to be holy and perfect, yet we always tell men to become holy and to seek perfection. We make it a duty to seek what is unattainable. We have the same paradox in the perfectibility of society. We shall never have a perfect social life, yet we must seek it with faith. We shall never abolish suffering. There will always be death and the empty chair and heart. There will always be the agony of love unreturned. Women will long for children and never press baby lips to their breast. Men will long for fame and miss it. Imperfect moral insight will work hurt in the best conceivable social order. The strong will always have the impulse to exert their strength, and no system can be devised which can keep them from crowding and jostling the weaker. Increased social refinement will bring increased sensitiveness to pain. An American may suffer as much distress through a social slight as a Russian peasant under the knout. At best there is always but an approximation to a perfect social order. The Kingdom of God is always but coming.

But every approximation to it is worth while. Every step toward personal purity and peace, though it only makes the consciousness of imperfection more poignant, carries its own exceeding great reward, and everlasting pilgrimage toward the Kingdom of God is better than contented stability in the tents of wickedness.

And sometimes the hot hope surges up that perhaps the long and slow climb may be ending. In the past the steps of our race toward progress have been short and feeble, and succeeded by long intervals of sloth and apathy. But is that necessarily to remain the rate of advance? In the intellectual life there has been an unprecedented leap forward during the last hundred years. Individually we are not more gifted than our grandfathers, but collectively we have wrought out more epoch-making discoveries and inventions in one century than the whole race in the untold centuries that have gone before. If the twentieth century could do for us in the control of social forces what the nineteenth did for us in the control of natural forces, our grandchildren would live in a society that would be justified in regarding our present social life as semibarbarous. Since the Reformation began to free the mind and to direct the force of religion toward morality, there has been a perceptible increase of speed. Humanity is gaining in elasticity and capacity for change, and every gain in general intelligence, in organizing capacity, in physical and moral soundness, and especially in responsiveness to ideal motives, again increases the ability to advance without disastrous reactions. The swiftness of evolution in our own country proves the immense latent perfectibility in human nature.

Last May a miracle happened. At the beginning of the week the fruit trees bore brown and greenish buds. At the end of the week they were robed in bridal garments of blossom. But for weeks and months the sap had been rising and distending the cells and maturing the tissues which were half ready in the fall before. The swift unfolding was the culmination of a long process. Perhaps these nineteen centuries of Christian influence have been a long preliminary stage of growth, and now the flower and fruit are almost here. If at this juncture we can rally sufficient religious faith and moral strength to snap the bonds of evil and turn the present unparalleled economic and intellectual resources of humanity to the harmonious development of a true social life, the generations yet unborn will mark this as that great day of the Lord for which the ages waited, and count us blessed for sharing in the apostolate that proclaimed it.

* II *

The Social Meaning of the Lord's Prayer

*I*N 1908, Theodore Roosevelt, who would relinquish the presidency on March 4, 1909, appointed a Commission on Conservation and one on Country Life. In 1909, Tennessee passed a state-wide prohibition law. Henry Ford advertised a six-cylinder automobile and the Wright brothers received a gold medal from President Taft. Orville Wright made a new record—he remained in the air in a plane one hour, one minute, and forty seconds.

The financial panic of late 1907 was followed by unemployment. Newspaper editorials were not patient with those out of work. But among sociologists and social workers, and a small minority of social-minded ministers, poverty in America was being discovered, described, and discussed.

Women smoking on their way to the opera drew a headline in the New York Herald. This break with tradition was regarded as an aspect of the shattering of national moral standards and some restaurants immediately placarded a rule against smoking by women.

Motion pictures were receiving attention. There was talk about the need for censoring them. Short movies in a one-hour program were often interspersed with invitations to the audience to join in singing popular songs.

Clergymen received public attention for various activities. The Reverend A. A. King and three companions made a trip around the world in forty-one days and eight hours. Cardinal Gibbons of Baltimore denounced the aims and methods of the prohibitionists. However, the Protestant churches became more and more active in their co-operation with the Anti-Saloon League.

Books widely read by people in the 1908–10 period included Trail

30

of the Lonesome Pine by John Fox, Jr.; The Calling of Dan Matthews and The Winning of Barbara Worth by Harold Bell Wright; The Rosary by Mrs. Florence Barclay; When a Man Marries by Mary Roberts Rinehart; The Silver Horde by Rex Beach; The Harvester by Gene Stratton Porter; Dawn O'Hara by Edna Ferber; Out-of-Doors in the Holy Land by Henry Van Dyke. Ministers outread their parishioners in theology but seldom in other literature.

The churches were still interested in temperance, missions, informal recreation for young people's societies, evangelistic campaigns. In some quarters one of the great issues was whether the congregation should use individual cups or a common cup when serving the wine of the holy communion. An attendant issue, by-product of the stirring campaigns for prohibition, was whether wine or unfermented grape juice should be used. Many congregations changed to grape juice. Strict Sabbath observance continued to be advocated, and middle-of-the-road Protestants opposed the on-rush of continental ideas of Sabbath observance.

In national circles church conventions began to make pronouncements on social issues. The Methodist Episcopal Church and the newly organized Federal Council of Churches were noting the crucial social problems in the cities and the demands of organized labor for the elementary right to organize. They adopted "social ideals" which opposed child labor, advocated fair wages and the right of both employees and employers to organize. In the Outlook, then a prominent weekly widely read by Protestants, Lyman Abbott recognized critical study of the Bible and advocated social action by churches in relation to the social crises of the day. The various pronouncements probably affected the policies of the local churches only slightly but ministers read them and while they did not share them with their congregations, and sometimes found themselves confused, they were stirred to thought. They wished to do something effective in relation to social needs, even when they did not know how.

In Rochester a busy and beloved man continued the unconventional tenor of his way. In November, 1908, Walter Rauschenbusch joined with Paul Moore Strayer and Henry H. Stebbins in serving as ministers of the People's Sunday Evening Service that met in the National Theater. They held mass meetings for "thinking people" who had lost contact with the Church. In addition to the forum, they organized an office to find jobs for the unemployed, and a personal counseling service for those with "religious doubts." By this time Rauschenbush was being widely quoted and was active as a special lecturer in churches,

YMCA's, the labor unions, the theological seminaries. He once sent out a letter to the "little churches" of his denomination, the Northern (now American) Baptist Convention, offering to lecture to them, his service "of course, to be entirely free."

"When traveling on railway trains alone, I used to meditate on the life problems of the people I saw," Walter Rauschenbusch once told his biographer, Dores Sharpe. "I then would shut out of my mind everything but the needs of those people. I imagine that my prayers were the fruitage of a real mystical withdrawal into communion with God."

There is no doubt but that Rauschenbusch was both mystic and social prophet. Believing that religion should be both individual and social, he found the religious expression of his day in the groove of a rigid individualism. He did not deprecate personal religion—he simply wished it to overflow into the social order, to create a social awakening, and thus to become religion high and true.

In 1909, two years after the publication of the first major book in English, Christianity and the Social Crisis, there appeared in England the book of prayers, Prayers of the Social Awakening. In 1910, Pilgrim Press of Boston brought out an American edition. The prayers, then collected in permanent form, had been written earlier under various circumstances, many of them having appeared month by month in the American Magazine. The author noted in a preface to the collection, "The response to them showed that there is a great craving for a religious expression of the new social feeling."

The new social purpose stirring in the world was "enlarging and transforming our whole conception of the meaning of Christianity." The Bible was speaking "a new and living language." The older tasks of the Church were taking on "a new significance, and vastly larger tasks are emerging as from the mists of a new morning." "Social Christianity is adding to the variety of religious experience. . . ."

These new emotions were not, thought Rauschenbusch, finding expression through conventional church liturgies and devotional manuals. "We need to blaze new paths to God for the feet of modern men." His "little book" was "an attempt in this direction." He foresaw objections to his method and his language, but he felt that "if the moral demands of our higher social thought could find adequate expression in prayer, it would have a profound influence on the social movement."

The article that follows here in full was Rauschenbusch's introduction. A selection of the prayers is given below.

*

THE Lord's Prayer is recognized as the purest expression of the mind of Jesus. It crystallizes his thoughts. It conveys the atmosphere of his childlike trust in the Father. It gives proof of the transparent clearness and peace of his soul.

It first took shape as a protest against the wordy flattery with which men tried to wheedle their gods. He demanded simplicity and sincerity in all expressions of religion, and offered this as an example of the straightforwardness with which men might deal with their Father. Hence the brevity and conciseness of it:

In praying use not vain repetitions, as the Gentiles do: for they think that they shall be heard for their much speaking. Be not therefore like unto them: for your Father knoweth what things ye have need of before ye ask him. After this manner therefore pray ye:
Our Father who art in heaven,
Hallowed be thy name.
Thy kingdom come.
Thy will be done, as in heaven, so on earth.
Give us this day our daily bread.
And forgive us our debts, as we also have forgiven our debtors.
And bring us not into temptation, but deliver us from the evil one.[1]

The Lord's Prayer is so familiar to us that few have stopped to understand it. The general tragedy of misunderstanding which has followed Jesus throughout the centuries has frustrated the purpose of his model prayer also. He gave it to stop vain repetitions, and it has been turned into a contrivance for incessant repetition.

The churches have employed it for their ecclesiastical ritual. Yet it is not ecclesiastical. There is no hint in it of the Church, the ministry, the doctrines of theology, or the sacraments—though the Latin Vulgate has turned the petition for the daily bread into a prayer for the "supersubstantial bread" of the sacrament.

It has also been used for the devotions of the personal religious life. It is, indeed, profoundly personal. But its deepest significance for the individual is revealed only when he dedicates his personality to the vaster purposes of the Kingdom of God, and approaches all his personal problems from that point of view. Then he enters both into the real meaning of the Lord's Prayer, and into the spirit of the Lord himself.

[1] Matt. 6:7–13 (American Revision).

The Lord's Prayer is part of the heritage of social Christianity which has been appropriated by men who have had little sympathy with its social spirit. It belongs to the equipment of the soldiers of the Kingdom of God. I wish to claim it here as the great charter of all social prayers.

When he bade us say, "Our Father," Jesus spoke from that consciousness of human solidarity which was a matter of course in all his thinking. He compels us to clasp hands in spirit with all our brothers and thus to approach the Father together. This rules out all selfish isolation in religion. Before God no man stands alone. Before the All-seeing he is surrounded by the spiritual throng of all to whom he stands related near and far, all whom he loves or hates, whom he serves or oppresses, whom he wrongs or saves. We are one with our fellow-men in all our needs. We are one in our sin and our salvation. To recognize that oneness is the first step toward praying the Lord's Prayer aright. That recognition is also the foundation of social Christianity.

The three petitions with which the prayer begins express the great desire which was fundamental in the heart and mind of Jesus: "Hallowed be thy name. Thy kingdom come. Thy will be done, as in heaven, so on earth." Together they express his yearning faith in the possibility of a reign of God on earth in which his name shall be hallowed and his will be done. They look forward to the ultimate perfection of the common life of humanity on this earth, and pray for the divine revolution which is to bring that about.

There is no request here that we be saved from earthliness and go to heaven which has been the great object of churchly religion. We pray here that heaven may be duplicated on earth through the moral and spiritual transformation of humanity, both in its personal units and its corporate life. No form of religion has ever interpreted this prayer aright which did not have a loving understanding for the plain daily relations of men, and a living faith in their possible spiritual nobility.

And no man has outgrown the crude selfishness of religious immaturity who has not followed Jesus in setting this desire for the social salvation of mankind ahead of all personal desires. The desire for the Kingdom of God precedes and outranks everything else in religion, and forms the tacit presupposition of all our wishes for ourselves. In fact, no one has a clear right to ask for bread for his body or strength for his soul, unless he has identified his will with this all-embracing purpose of God, and intends to use the vitality of body and soul in the attainment of that end.

With that understanding we can say that the remaining petitions deal with personal needs.

Among these the prayer for the daily bread takes first place. Jesus was never as "spiritual" as some of his later followers. He never forgot or belittled the elemental need of men for bread. The fundamental place which he gives to this petition is a recognition of the economic basis of life.

But he lets us pray only for the bread that is needful, and for that only when it becomes needful. The conception of what is needful will expand as human life develops. But this prayer can never be used to cover luxuries that debilitate, nor accumulations of property that can never be used but are sure to curse the soul of the holder with the diverse diseases of mammonism.

In this petition, too, Jesus compels us to stand together. We have to ask in common for our daily bread. We sit at the common table in God's great house, and the supply of each depends on the security of all. The more society is socialized, the clearer does that fact become, and the more just and humane its organization becomes, the more will that recognition be at the bottom of all our institutions. As we stand thus in common, looking up to God for our bread, every one of us ought to feel the sin and shame of it if he habitually takes more than his fair share and leaves others hungry that he may surfeit. It is inhuman, irreligious, and indecent.

The remaining petitions deal with the spiritual needs. Looking backward, we see that our lives have been full of sin and failure, and we realize the need of forgiveness. Looking forward, we tremble at the temptations that await us and pray for deliverance from evil.

In these prayers for the inner life, where the soul seems to confront God alone, we should expect to find only individualistic religion. But even here the social note sounds clearly.

This prayer will not permit us to ask for God's forgiveness without making us affirm that we have forgiven our brothers and are on a basis of brotherly love with all men: "Forgive us our debts, as we also have forgiven our debtors." We shall have to be socially right if we want to be religiously right. Jesus will not suffer us to be pious toward God and merciless toward men.

In the prayer "Lead us not into temptation" we feel the human trembling of fear. Experience has taught us our frailty. Every man can see certain contingencies just a step ahead of him and knows that his moral capacity for resistance would collapse hopelessly if he were placed in these situations. Therefore Jesus gives voice to our inarticulate plea to God not to bring us into such situations.

But such situations are created largely by the social life about us. If the society in which we move is rank with sexual looseness, or full of the suggestiveness and solicitations of alcoholism; if our business life is such that we have to lie and cheat and be cruel in order to live and prosper; if our political organization offers an ambitious man the alternative of betraying the public good or of being thwarted and crippled in all his efforts, then the temptations are created in which men go under, and society frustrates the prayer we utter to God. No church can interpret this petition intelligently which closes its mind to the debasing or invigorating influence of the spiritual environment furnished by society. No man can utter this petition without conscious or unconscious hypocrisy who is helping to create the temptations in which others are sure to fall.

The words "Deliver us from the evil one" have in them the ring of battle. They bring to mind the incessant grapple between God and the permanent and malignant powers of evil in humanity. To the men of the first century that meant Satan and his host of evil spirits who ruled in the oppressive, extortionate, and idolatrous powers of Rome. Today the original spirit of that prayer will probably be best understood by those who are pitted against the terrible powers of organized covetousness and institutionalized oppression.

Thus the Lord's Prayer is the great prayer of social Christianity. It is charged with what we call "social consciousness." It assumes the social solidarity of men as a matter of course. It recognizes the social basis of all moral and religious life even in the most intimate personal relations to God.

It is not the property of those whose chief religious aim is to pass through an evil world in safety, leaving the world's evil unshaken. Its dominating thought is the moral and religious transformation of mankind in all its social relations. It was left us by Jesus, the great initiator of the Christian revolution; and it is the rightful property of those who follow his banner in the conquest of the world.

* III *

Christianizing the Social Order

*I*N 1911 postal savings banks were opened in every state of the Union amid much discussion of appropriate public enterprise and function. How far should the government go? The Supreme Court announced the dissolution of the Standard Oil Company. Soon came editorials on the meaning of this action for a nation devoted to private enterprise and freedom. What should be the nature and extent of public guidance and regulation of the corporations?

In 1912 the textile workers of Lawrence, Massachusetts, began a long and bitter strike, and people pondered the right of strikers and whether there could eventually be means of conciliation. The Supreme Court ordered the dissolution of the merger of Union Pacific and Southern Pacific Railroads.

Ten thousand suffragettes marched in the streets of New York. Norman Hapgood, then editor of Collier's, wrote an editorial on the significance of the motion picture.

Popular songs were: "Oceana Roll," "Mysterious Rag," "Alexander's Rag Time Band," "That Raggy Rag," "You Great Big Beautiful Doll."

Burton Stevenson compiled the Home Book of Verse. Theodore Dreiser's The Financier was not on any best-seller list. In addition to books by Harold Bell Wright, Gene Stratton Porter, and Edna Ferber, best sellers included The Common Law by Robert W. Chambers; The Iron Woman by Margaret Deland; The Squirrel Cage by Dorothy Canfield Fisher; Riders of the Purple Sage by Zane Grey; Love's Coming of Age by Edward Carpenter.

In politics, Theodore Roosevelt became more and more displeased with the way William Howard Taft conducted his office. In 1910 while T.R. was on safari in Africa Mr. Taft had removed Gifford Pinchot from the Forest Service. In 1912, Mr. Roosevelt received a formal request from seven Republican governors to run for President, and threw his hat into the ring. Running into a violent dispute with the leaders of the Republican National Convention, he and his followers bolted and formed a Progressive party. Giving up his battle to modernize the Republican party, or to reform it from within, he fought it from without, letting loose all his powers as a political preacher against those in the fold of which he had been a member. On October 14, 1912, he was shot while speaking in Milwaukee but the bullet lodged almost harmlessly in his body and he soon resumed his campaign. The party split insured the election of Woodrow Wilson.

Woodrow Wilson had been elected governor of New Jersey in 1910. He had published The New Freedom, in which he had outlined his own liberal policies, alleging that government should serve to release the creative energies of a free people. He, too, vigorously opposed monopolies. In the Democratic National Convention of 1912, William Jennings Bryan, still a popular and influential figure on the prairies and elsewhere, was the main power that broke the deadlock between the forces of Champ Clark and those of Woodrow Wilson.

Rauschenbusch read the speeches of Bryan and Theodore Roosevelt among many other works on the social issues of the day. When he had written Christianity and the Social Crisis he thought he had delivered himself upon the issues. But the prophet's pen was not to be silent. He was appealed to for more and more specifics in the way of program. There was waiting and groping among the ministers who conducted their conventional church services, collected money for missions, and approved single and simple acts of social service. What about broad social reform? What about preaching, pronouncing, and acting? How much should the churches undertake? How much reform would lay people approve and support?

Rauschenbusch's social philosophy had already taken form in the pastorate in New York prior to 1897, and in his participation in the Baptist Congress for the discussion of current questions. It was a blend of his studies and conclusions from his reading of history, religion, and sociology, and the social reformers. His social interest probably did not come out of his early environment. But in the pastorate, meeting human needs, he sought the aid of the writers and thinkers. We do not know when he adopted the socialist ideal (without joining the party), but by 1889 he was editing a Christian Socialist magazine. In 1907 he studied intensively the socialist movements of Europe, along with other economic movements such as the Rochdale co-operatives.

Dores Sharpe, Rauschenbusch's biographer, writes that there were two important stands in the booklet's social philosophy—one, the concept of the Kingdom of God; two, the ideal of socialism. They were constantly interwoven in Rauschenbusch's thinking and were brought into focus when he wrote for the Church and the world his concept of the revolutionary destiny of Christianity in social terms.

The theme of the revolutionary destiny of Christianity was developed in the book, Christianizing the Social Order (New York, The Macmillan Company, 1912), containing the substance of two series of lectures previously delivered. Here Rauschenbusch taught in specifics with respect to what the social problems were and what the message of Christianity was. Here he distilled and crystallized all the experience and thought of the days of the pastorate near Hell's Kitchen, all his biblical study, and all his wide range of reading in Christian tradition and the writings of a large number of social scientists and reformers. Patently he influenced and was influenced by Jane Addams and many others who shared his concerns.

As a result of his experience and reading he came to this conclusion: "We must begin at both ends simultaneously. We must change our economic system in order to preserve our conscience and our religious faith; we must renew and strengthen our religion in order to be able to change our economic system."

The compiler's notes on the situation in the churches given with the excerpts from Christianity and the Social Crisis, above, also apply here. The book of 1912 did not attain the same popularity as the one of 1907. But today in perspective it must be regarded as one of the more important of the prophet's thrusts. It had a great influence on many individuals still living, who ponder the extent to which it may have moved other persons and the institutions of religion which usually resist the changes advocated by its prophets. There now appears evidence of another turning from individualism toward social religion and social concern.

Major portions of three chapters that at least illustrate the main direction of the book are given here.

*

INTRODUCTION

WHEN Christianity and the Social Crisis was published in 1907, I thought I had said all that God had given me to say on our social problems, and might henceforth with a clear conscience leave that line of work to those who carry less handicap than I do. So I went to Europe for a year and devoted myself to the historical studies which are my professional duty and my intellectual satisfaction.

But meanwhile the social awakening of our nation had set in like an equinoctial gale in March, and when I came home, I found myself caught in the tail of the storm. *Christianity and the Social Crisis* had won popular approval far beyond my boldest hopes, and the friends of the book drew me, in spite of myself, into the public discussion of social questions. Naturally my mind worked on problems which had been raised in my book, but had not really been taken in hand there. I had urged a moral reorganization of social institutions, a christianizing of public morality. Men asked: "What must we do? And what must we undo? What social ideal should guide us? What methods can we safely use in realizing it?" The most varied audiences followed the discussion of these problems with an intensity of interest that was quite new to me. Without the spiritual co-operation and stimulus of others this book would never have been written.

In 1910 and 1911 I had the honor of delivering the Earl Lectures at the Pacific Theological Seminary at Berkeley, California, and the Merrick Lectures at Ohio Wesleyan University. The latter lectureship carried the obligation of publishing the lectures in book form. I take this opportunity to express my obligation to the Faculties and Officers of both institutions for courtesies which I shall never forget, and for providing the incentive to work out my thought in written form. These two lecture courses created the nucleus of this book; the form, however, and much of the contents are new.

The subject of the book needs no such apology as is implied in the foregoing statements. If there is any bigger or more pressing subject for the mind of a Christian man to handle, I do not know of it. The problem of christianizing the social order welds all the tasks of practical Christianity with the highest objects of statesmanship. That the actual results of our present social order are in acute contradiction to the Christian conceptions of justice and brotherhood is realized by every man who thinks at all. But where do the sources of our wrongs lie hidden? What has wrought such deadly results from a civilization that has such wonderful promises of good? How can we cease to produce evil in despite of our right intentions? How can the fundamental structure of society be conformed to the moral demands of the Christian spirit?

The book describes the present social awakening in the organizations of religion. Outsiders misjudge the part which the churches are taking in the impending social transformation because they are ignorant of the quiet revolution that is going on in the spirit and aims of the American churches. Few, probably, even of those who are taking an active part in their social awakening, realize fully the far-reaching importance of this great historic movement.

The christianizing of the social order was the very aim with which Christianity set out. That aim has long been submerged and almost forgotten, but it has re-emerged simultaneously with the rise of modern life, and now demands a reckoning with every religious intellect, offering us all a richer synthesis of truth and a more distinctively Christian type of religious experience.

[This book] subjects our present social order to a moral analysis in order to determine what is Christian in the structure of society, and what is not. This traverses some of the ground covered in my previous book, but from new angles. In spite of its critical character the net results of the analysis, to me at least, are immensely cheering.

The unregenerate elements of our social organization are not quietly waiting till we get ready to reform them, but are actively invading God's country and devastating the moral achievements built up by centuries of Christian teaching and sacrifice.

I have tried to trace in advance those fundamental lines of moral evolution along which society must move in order to leave its inhumanities behind and to emerge in a social order that will institutionalize the Christian convictions of the worth of manhood and the solidarity of mankind.

Finally, [the book] suggests the methods of advance, the personal and social action by which our present conditions can be molded into a juster and happier community life in which the Christian spirit shall be more free to work its will.

If this book was to be written at all, it had to deal searchingly with the great collective sins of our age. Evangelism always seeks to create a fresh conviction of guilt as a basis for a higher righteousness, and this book is nothing if it is not a message of sin and salvation. But its purpose is not denunciation. It is wholly constructive. Of *Christianity and the Social Crisis* it has been said that it is a book without any hate in it. So far as I know my own soul that is true of this book, too. I have written it as a follower of Jesus Christ. My sole desire has been to summon the Christian passion for justice and the Christian powers of love and mercy to do their share in redeeming our social order from its inherent wrongs.

*

WANTED: A FAITH FOR A TASK

+A GREAT task demands a great faith. To live a great life a man needs a great cause to which he can surrender, something divinely large and engrossing for which he can live and, if need be, die. A great religious faith will lift him out of his narrow grooves and make him the inspired instrument of the universal will of God. It is the point at which the mind of man coincides with the mind of the Eternal. A vital faith will gradually saturate a man's whole life and master not only his conscious energies, but his subconscious drifts. The religious revolution in Paul's life was due to a new faith which seized him and made him over, and ever after he knew that a man is justified by a faith more than by any doings. He had made proof of the fact.

Our entire generation needs a faith, for it is confronting the mightiest task ever undertaken consciously by any generation of men. Our civilization is passing through a great historic transition. We are at the parting of the ways. The final outcome may be the decay and extinction of Western civilization, or it may be a new epoch in the evolution of the race, compared with which our present era will seem like a modified barbarism. We now have such scientific knowledge of social laws and forces, of economics, of history that we can intelligently mold and guide the evolution in which we take part. Our fathers cowered before the lightning; we have subdued it to our will. Former generations were swept along more or less blindly toward a hidden destiny; we have reached the point where we can make history make us. Have we the will to match our knowledge? Can we marshal the moral forces capable of breaking what must be broken, and then building what must be built? What spiritual hosts can God line up to rout the Devil in the battle of Armageddon?

Our moral efficiency depends on our religious faith. The force of will, of courage, of self-sacrifice liberated by a living religious faith is so incalculable, so invincible, that nothing is impossible when that power enters the field. The author of the greatest revolution in history made the proposition that even the slighest amount of faith is competent to do the unbelievable; faith as tiny as a mustard seed can blast away mountains.

"Every great revolution demands a great idea to be its center of action; to furnish it with both lever and fulcrum for the work it has to do." [1] What great idea has the Christian Church which will serve as the religious lever and fulcrum for the engineering task of the present generation? What great faith has it which will inspire the religious minds of our modern world in the regeneration of society?

The chief purpose of the Christian Church in the past has been the salvation of individuals. But the most pressing task of the present is not individualistic. Our business is to make over an antiquated and immoral economic system; to get rid of laws, customs, maxims, and philosophies inherited from an evil and despotic past; to create just and brotherly relations between great groups and classes of society; and thus to lay a social foundation on which modern men individually can live and work in a fashion that will not outrage all the better elements in them. Our inherited Christian faith dealt with individuals; our present task deals with society.

The Christian Church in the past has taught us to do our work with our eyes fixed on another world and a life to come. But the business before us is concerned with refashioning this present world, making this earth clean and sweet and habitable.

Here is the problem for all religious minds: we need a great faith to serve as a spiritual basis for the tremendous social task before us, and the working creed of our religion, in the form in which it has come down to us, has none. Its theology is silent or stammers where we most need a ringing and dogmatic message. It has no adequate answer to the fundamental moral questions of our day. It has manifestly furnished no sufficient religious motives to bring the unregenerate portions of our social order under the control of the Christian law. Its hymns, its ritual, its prayers, its books of devotion, are so devoid of social thought that the most thrilling passions of our generation lie in us half stifled for lack of religious utterance. The whole scheme of religion which tradition has handed down to us was not devised for such ends as we now have in hand and is inadequate for them. We need a new foundation for Christian thought.

The straits of the churches in their present social awakening are both interesting and pathetic. They are in the position of a middle-aged American in Paris suddenly plunged into trouble with the police, and feeling around in his mind for the French vocabulary he forgot when he was a sophomore.

Twenty-five years ago the social wealth of the Bible was almost undiscovered to most of us. We used to plow it six inches deep for crops and never dreamed that mines of anthracite were hidden down below. Even Jesus talked like an individualist in those days and seemed to

[1] Mazzini, "Faith and the Future," in his *Essays*, Camelot Edition.

repudiate the social interest when we interrogated him. He said his kingdom was not of this world; the things of God had nothing to do with the things of Caesar; the poor we would always have with us; and his ministers must not be judges and dividers when Labor argued with Capital about the division of the inheritance. Today he has resumed the spiritual leadership of social Christianity, of which he was the founder. It is a new tribute to his mastership that the social message of Jesus was the first great possession which social Christianity redis-covered. A course of lectures on the social teachings of Jesus is usually the earliest symptom that the social awakening has arrived. Is it another compliment to the undischarged force of his thoughts that we handle them so gingerly, as if they were boxed explosives? We have also worked out the social ideas of the Old Testament prophets. But that is about as far as the popular comprehension of the Bible has gone. We have let Paul severely alone. The Apocalypse is not yet printed in red, as it might be. Few commentaries show any streaks of social insight. We have no literature that introduces the ordinary reader to the whole Bible from the social point of view.

In its systematic doctrinal teaching the Church is similarly handi-capped. It is trying old tools to see if they will fit the new job. It has done splendidly in broadening certain principles developed under re-ligious individualism and giving them a social application. But more is needed.

With true Christian instinct men have turned to the Christian law of love as the key to the situation. If we all loved our neighbor, we should "treat him right," pay him a living wage, give sixteen ounces to the pound, and not charge so much for beef. But this appeal as-sumes that we are still living in the simple personal relations of the good old times, and that every man can do the right thing when he wants to do it. But suppose a businessman would be glad indeed to pay his young women the twelve dollars a week which they need for a decent living, but all his competitors are paying from seven dollars down to five dollars. Shall he love himself into bankruptcy? In a time of industrial depression shall he employ men whom he does not need? And if he does, will his five loaves feed the five thousand unemployed that break his heart with their hungry eyes? If a man owns a hundred shares of stock in a great corporation, how can his love influence its wage scale with that puny stick? The old advice of love breaks down before the hugeness of modern relations. We might as well try to start a stranded ocean liner with the oar which poled our old dory from the mud banks many a time. It is indeed love that we want, but it is socialized love. Blessed be the love that holds the cup of water to thirsty lips. We can never do without the plain affection of man to man. But what we most need today is not the love that will break its back drawing water for a growing factory town from a well that was meant to supply a village, but a love so large and intelligent that it will persuade an ignorant people to build a system of waterworks up in the hills, and that will get after the thoughtless farmers who contaminate the brooks with typhoid bacilli, and after the lumber concern that is denuding the watershed of its forests. We want a new avatar of love.

The Church has also put a new stress on the doctrine of stewardship, hoping to cure the hard selfishness of our commercial life by quickening the sense of responsibility in men of wealth. This also is wholly in the right direction, but here, too, the Church is still occupying the mental position of the old régime. The word "stewardship" itself comes down to us from an age of great landed proprietors. It has an antique dignity that guarantees it as harmless. The modern equivalent would be trusteeship. But a trustee does not own; he merely manages. If he mismanages or diverts trust funds to his own use, he is legally liable. If that is what we mean when we preach stewardship, we should be denying the private property rights on which capitalism rests, and morally expropriating the owners. In that case we ought to see to it that this moral conception of property was embodied in the laws, and that the people would get orderly legal redress against stewards who have misused their trusteeship. That would mean a sort of Recall for businessmen. But in fact the Church puts no such cutting edge on the doctrine. It uses it to appeal to the conscience of powerful individuals to make them realize that they are accountable to God for the way they spend their money. The doctrine is not yet based on modern democratic feeling and on economic knowledge about the sources of modern wealth. It calls for no fundamental change in economic distribution, but simply encourages faithful disbursement of funds. That is not enough for our modern needs.

The Golden Rule is often held up as a sufficient solution of the social problem. "If only all men would act on the Golden Rule!" But curiously enough men find it hard to act on it, even when they indorse and praise it. There seem to be temptations of gain or of fear in our modern life before which our good intentions collapse. But even as a standard to guide our moral intelligence the Golden Rule is not really adequate for our needs. It is a wonderfully practical guide in all simple, personal relations. It appeals to our imagination to put ourselves in the other man's place and thus discover how we ought to treat him. It turns the flank of our selfishness, and compels that highly developed instinct in us to put itself into the service of love. Like the span measure of our right hand we can carry this rule about with us wherever we go, but it is hardly long enough to survey and lay out the building site of the New Jerusalem. Jesus probably did not intend it for more than an elementary method of figuring our duty.

The Church has also revived the thought of following Jesus in daily conduct, living over again the life of Christ, and doing in all things as he would do in our place. That has been an exceedingly influential thought in Christian history. In the life of St. Francis and his brotherhood, in the radical sects, and in single radiant lives it has produced social forces of immense power. In our own time the books of Mr. Charles M. Sheldon have set it forth with winning spirit, and we have seen thousands of young people trying for a week to live as Jesus would. But it is so high a law that only consecrated individuals can follow it permanently and intelligently, and even they may submit to it only in the high tide of their spiritual life. To most men the demand to live as Jesus would, is mainly useful to bring home the fact that it is hard to live a Christlike life in a mammonistic society. It convicts our social order of sin, but it does not reconstruct it.

These are all truly religious ideas, drawn from the teaching of Jesus himself, and very effective in sweetening and ennobling our personal relations. But they set up no ideal of human society, demand no transformation of social institutions, create no collective enthusiasms, and furnish no doctrinal basis for a public morality. They have not grown antiquated, and never will. But every step in the evolution of modern society makes them less adequate for its religious needs. The fact that the Church is leaning so hard on them at present shows how earnestly it is trying to meet the present need, and also how scanty is the equipment with which it confronts the new social task.

So we return to the question: What is the religious basis for the task of christianizing and regenerating the social order? Suppose that a Christian man feels a throbbing compassion and fellow-feeling for the people, and a holy anger against the institutionalized wrong that is stunting and brutalizing their lives, converting the children of God into slaves of Mammon. Suppose that he feels this so strongly that he hardly cares what becomes of his own soul if only he can help his nation and race. Suppose that a whole generation is coming vaguely to feel that way. What great word of faith does historic Christianity offer to express and hallow and quicken this spiritual passion which is so evidently begotten of the spirit of Christ? Must he go to materialistic socialism to find a dogmatic faith large enough to house him, and intellectual food nutritious enough to feed his hunger? Thousands have left the Church and have gone to socialism, not to shake off a faith, but to get a faith.

I raise this challenge because I believe Christianity can meet it. My purpose is not critical, but wholly constructive. If I did not believe in the vitality and adaptability of the Christian faith, I should sit down with Job on the ashes and keep silence.

But let no one take the challenge lightly. It points to no superficial flaw in the working machinery of the Church, but to the failure of our religious ideas to connect with our religious needs, and that is fundamental. Religion, to have power over an age, must satisfy the highest moral and religious desires of that age. If it lags behind, and presents outgrown conceptions of life and duty, it is no longer in the full sense the Gospel.

*

"THE POWERS OF THE COMING AGE"

WE HAVE seen that the social intuitions of the Christian spirit are confirmed and verified by history. Our fathers moved in the same direction as we.

Our ethical foresight is also verified by the young life of our own times. The new economic order is even now growing up and maturing among us, and we can begin to discern its fundamental bent.

Our age is like a family circle in which three generations are grouped around the same fireplace: the grandparents who ruled the past, the parents who are carrying the burdens of the present, and the children who are growing up to take their place. None of the three generations realizes how swiftly they are moving across the stage of life. So three economic orders are combining to make up the total of modern life: the precapitalistic which is passing away, the capitalistic which is in the flush of its strength, and the collectivistic which is still immature. Most farmers, some mechanics, and many small business men are still to some extent living according to the methods and the spirit of the age before capitalism. Capitalism, both in its competitive and its monopolistic form, is dominating our business, our legislation, our institutions, and our thought, and thinks it always has been and always will be. But on all hands a new order is growing up, young, vigorous, and clamorous, eager to inherit the house and run it in its own way.

Each of these three stages of social evolution is affected by the other two. None is able to express its peculiar spirit and genius in logical severity and simplicity. But there is a deep difference discernible, not only between their economic methods, but between their ethical spirit and their philosophy of life, and those social movements and organizations which most distinctly belong to the future, most clearly embody the characteristics of the Christian economic order. This is another corroboration of our faith. I have no space for an extended study of the embryonic social organizations of the future order, but shall present a few evidences to back my claim.

Few people in America, unless they have given special attention to the matter, as yet have any idea of the scope and importance of the modern co-operative associations. In Europe they have developed by thousands, especially since 1870. The network of these associations has become an economic and social fact of first-class importance, and in some countries, such as Belgium, Denmark, and Ireland, they have begun to change the economic and social character of the nation. There are co-operative retail stores, associated in large wholesale associations which manufacture for their own market; building and loan associations to furnish cheap credit; purchasing associations to buy raw material for mechanics, or seeds, fertilizers, and agricultural implements for farmers; societies to sell handicraft products or market-garden truck and farm products; co-operative mills, bakeries, slaughterhouses, creameries, cheese factories, and grain elevators.

Their immediate aim is to save the middleman's profit for their members, to insure them clean and unadulterated goods and honest weights and measures, to save them from the parasitic trickery of the petty middleman and the usury of the money shark who exploit the poor, to train their people to frugality by cash payments and small savings, and to secure for the working class and the lower middle class some share in social wealth and profit. Every co-operative association encounters the same initial difficulties as any other business concern. They have to meet the most efficient survivors of capitalistic competition. They usually start with little capital and less experience, a double lack that would almost certainly be fatal to an ordinary business undertaking. There have been many failures, especially at first before the conditions for success had been worked out by experience. In some fields of enterprise they have not succeeded. But taking them in the large, they have demonstrated their economic fitness just as convincingly as the corporation. Yet they rest on a different moral basis.

The corporation is a product of the business class and takes its psychological coloring from that class. The co-operative is an organization of the earning classes, the industrial workers, the small farmers, and the lower business class, and it draws its strength from their peculiar moral qualities. The corporation is an association of capital; money counts in it; the members vote by the number of shares they hold; the small stockholder is practically a cipher in the management. The co-operative is an association of men; one man has one vote, regardless of the number of shares held. They have learned to appreciate the technical efficiency of salaried officers, but their directors give unpaid service for love of the cause, and the general business meeting of the members is the real power, at least in the smaller associations. "The number of bankruptcies and defalcations by directorates and officials is infinitely smaller in the world of the co-operative associations than in the corporations and big private business concerns." [1] The capitalistic corporation is after profits; its stockholders have no use for the goods they help to produce except as they earn profit; it accepts the brute struggle for existence as the law of business. The co-operative has a far stronger sense of humanity; it thrives best where the sense of solidarity is stoutest; its abler members seek to lift the weaker with them as they rise to economic prosperity. They do try to save money; they do not try to exploit men to make money. They refrain from taking business away from the ordinary dealer by cutting the market prices, though they might, in many cases, drive them out of business. They distribute the benefits to those who have made actual use of the co-operative plant, and according to the amount of use they have made of it.

Thus the co-operative associations represent a new principle in economic life, clearly of higher ethical quality than the principle dominant in capitalism. They combine a wholesomely selfish desire to get ahead with genuine fraternal sympathy and solidarity, and the combination works and holds its own against the most efficient business concerns in those fields where the co-operatives have learned to master the situation. They have appropriated the business system and calculating keenness of capitalism, but they draw the lower classes whom capitalism has almost deprived of initiative into the management, and train them to industrial and moral efficiency. Their methods have been adapted from the joint stock company, but their spirit is drawn from the older communal organizations, from the new socialist hatred for exploiting methods, and from the depths of uncontaminated human nature. There is no prospect that the co-operative associations will displace capitalism, but they have a great future and no limit can be set to their possibilities. They have proved what a fund of good sense and ability lies unused in the lower classes. They have demonstrated the economic efficiency of fraternal co-operation. They are creating everywhere trained groups, capable of assuming larger responsibilities when the time comes, and a new spirit that can afford to look down on the exploiting spirit of capitalism. Thus the achievements of these humble co-operators are

[1] Schmoller, Volkswirtschaftslehre, I, 447.

the beginnings of a higher business morality. They are part of the newly forming tissue of a Christian social order and are one of "the powers of the coming age." [2]

The organizations of labor are also part of that new economic order which is growing up in the midst of capitalism.

From some points of view the unions are just as brutally commercial in their tactics as any capitalistic corporation. They sell labor wholesale as others sell goods, and they seize every advantage of the market as shrewdly and ruthlessly as any trust. But there are human and ethical values in trades unionism which put them on a different footing, and explain the wonderful hold which the unions have on the loyalty of the elite of the working class.

Wherever their influence reaches among the workers, they substitute the principle of solidarity for that of competitive selfishness. They train their members to stand together loyally and to sacrifice their private and immediate advantage for some larger benefit to be won for all. It is true, they seek the advantage only of their own group, and not directly of all society. But what class does? Few loyalties have been world wide. Even patriotism is a limited devotion, bounded by the nation. Christian love itself checks its pace when it crosses the threshold of its own particular Church. Why should we demand of one of the lowest classes, fighting on the borderland of poverty, an unselfish devotion to all society which the upper classes have never shown? The group selfishness of the unions is at least a larger and nobler selfishness than that of the strike breaker whom the public sentiment of capitalism praises and rewards. The capitalistic class finds it hard to understand the ethical value of the solidarity exhibited by organized labor, because commercial practices have fatally disintegrated its own capacity to stand together for similiar sacrifices.

When the unions demand a fixed minimum wage, a maximum working day, and certain reasonable conditions of labor as a security for health, safety, and continued efficiency, they are standing for human life against profits. With capitalism the dollor is the unit of all calculations; with unionism it is life. With capitalism the main purpose of industry is to make as large a profit as possible, and it makes the margin of life narrow in order to make the margin of profit wide. With unionism the purpose of industry is to support as large a number of workingmen's families in comfort as possible. Capitalism and union-

---

[2] See Holyoke, *History of Coöperation in England*; Beatrice Potter (Mrs. Sidney Webb), *The Coöperative Movement in Great Britain*; Acland and Jones, *Workingmen Coöperators*; Henry D. Lloyd, *Labor Copartnership*.

ism fail to understand each other because they revolve around a different axis.

We have seen that the perversities of our economic order force the businessmen into false positions. The workingmen are put in the wrong in the same way. Their noblest impulses often lead to actions that shock the moral judgment of outsiders. For instance, the sympathetic strike is condemned by law, by public opinion, and by the cautious prudence of the leaders of labor, yet the labor organizations are often quivering on the verge of it. And as a demonstration of altruism and solidarity it is sublime. Like the charge of the six hundred at Balaklava, it is not war, but it is magnificent. Thousands of men and women giving up their job, their slender hold on subsistence, imperiling the bread and butter of their families for the sake of men in another trade with whom they have only a distant economic connection, simply to help their fellows in a fight which they feel to be their own—where in the transactions of the business class, and where in church life do we find such heroic self-sacrifice of great bodies of men and women for a common cause?

Organized labor is blamed for limiting the pace of work in a shop and restraining the capable workers from doing their best. It surely seems dishonest for a workman not to give his employer the best work that is in him, and it levels the standard of work down below the maximum of efficiency. In a co-operative democracy of labor such a condition would indeed be against the common good and ethically intolerable, but as long as the workers are on the defensive against a superior force that seeks to get the maximum of labor from them for the minimum of reward, this unnatural condition may actually be moral. The men know by bitter experience that in some shops the pace set by the young and able is soon demanded of all and made compulsory by speeding up the machinery or cutting the price of piecework. The few may gain if the capable do their best, but the mass would lose. The older and slower workmen could not keep up at all; the strength of the others would be drained. Under such conditions the workers are in a moral dilemma, cornered between two wrongs or two duties. When they limit the pace of the capable, they enforce the law of solidarity: "Bear ye one another's burdens, and so fulfill the law of Christ." But with what right can the capitalist class blame them, which everywhere seeks to limit the output in order to maintain its monopoly prices? The Steel Trust fixing prices for all steel manufacturers by a gentleman's agreement, and a shop of workmen enforcing the "ca' canny" policy on all the men, are both doing the same thing. The Steel Trust does it to keep up its enormous profits. The workingmen do it to preserve their health against premature exhaustion, and in order to help the older men to hold their job. If there must be limitation of output, who has the better cause?

Labor unions are fighting organizations, and fighting always abridges personal liberty and stiffens the demand for obedience and subordination. In the long fight of labor the odds are nearly always against it, sometimes enormously so. The employers have the tremendous backing of property rights and the long wind given by large resources. The Law, which ought theoretically to be impartial, has always been made by the powerful classes. It used to treat the organization of workingmen as conspiracy, and still takes a grudging attitude toward demands which are clearly just. The battle of labor is fought by a few for all. Only a minority of the industrial workers is sufficiently strong economically, and sufficiently developed morally, to bear the strain of organized effort. Unorganized labor reaps the advantages of the sacrifices made by the unions, yet often thwarts their efforts and defeats the common cause. Bitterness, roughness, and violence are inevitable in such a conflict. The danger of tyranny is real enough. But underneath the grime of battle is the gleam of a higher purpose and law which these men are seeking to obey and to bring to victory. They are standing for the growth of democracy, for earned against unearned income, for the protection of human weakness against the pressure of profit, for the right of recreation, education, and love, and for the solidarity of the workers. They doubtless sin, but even the errors of labor are lovable compared with the errors of capitalism. The seed of a new social order is in them. They too belong to "the powers of the coming age."

The co-operative associations and the organizations of labor are practical efforts to secure immediate benefits for the persons who unite in these movements. Two other great movements, the single tax and socialism, offer no direct advantage to their supporters. Each is a missionary movement and bears a gospel of social salvation to our capitalistic age. I point to them here as proof that the moral and spiritual convictions on which a new social order will have to be based are gaining force and are even now preparing that new order.

"All the evils under which civilized people suffer can be traced back to private property in land as their cause." [3] All tyranny and exploitation is based on the control of the natural resources of the earth. Whoever owns the earth can exploit the people who live on it. In our industrial era the increase and concentration of population have enormously increased land values and enabled the owners of the land to levy a tribute on the working population beyond compute.

Wherever the demand for justice has become intelligent and thor-

[3] Zachariae, *Bücher vom Staat.*

ough, it has included a demand for the restoration of the land to the people in some form. But a continuous, world-wide agitation, based on a scientific theory, and offering a simple and practicable reform, has begun only with the man Henry George and his book, *Progress and Poverty*. Editorial wiseacres still keep on informing us that the Henry George movement failed. God grant all good men such failure! It failed in its first attempt to carry politics by storm, but it betook itself to the education of the public mind. Henceforth it distrusted party organization and put its faith in intellectual conviction. Its teachings dropped into the minds of the young and grew up with them. Now that the men who were young twenty-five years ago have come to maturity and influence, the teachings of Henry George are everywhere entering practical politics, though supported by the slenderest sort of organization. The budget of Lloyd George in 1910, which precipitated the constitutional revolution in England, was only the beginning of a movement to socialize the income from the land, and it is well understood that radical land taxation will be the next great step in the social revolution going on in Great Britain. Since 1900 a number of cities in Germany have been taxing the unearned increment whenever land is sold, and the tax proved so simple, painless, and profitable that the Imperial Government has begun to draw on the same source for its revenues. New Zealand has a local option law in taxation under which nearly a hundred municipalities derive their local expenses from land values exclusively. The young cities of the Canadian Northwest are doing the same. In several of our older States movements are on foot to deal with the housing question by gradually shifting taxation from improvements to land values, thus forcing idle land into use and encouraging building. The whole procedure and administration of taxation has been deeply affected by the spread of single tax convictions.

But this movement is not simply the propagation of a new tax device, but the proclamation of a new social order. It is the uncovering of the most fundamental form of unearned wealth, and a democratic protest against the economic aristocracy built up on the unearned increment. Scratch a single-taxer and you find a genuine democrat who can be depended on to oppose all other forms of unjust privilege. Tom L. Johnson, who was won from the aimless acquisition of riches to the service of the people by the gospel of Henry George, applied the insight gained from the single tax doctrine to the knotty relations between the American municipalities and the public service corporations. He was only a conspicuous example of a new generation of public men whose souls and intellects have been saved from the vice of unearned money by that doctrine, and who are now occupied with the practical problems of political and economic democracy. The single tax movement has not appealed to the working class as powerfully as socialism, but it is a system of thought exactly adapted to middle-class intellectuals and to religious individualists. I owe my own first awakening to the world of social problems to the agitation of Henry George in 1886, and wish here to record my lifelong debt to this single-minded apostle of a great truth.

Socialism, on the other hand, has laid hold of the industrial working class with the grip of destiny. It promises these propertyless men that they shall once more own the tools of their work, share in the profit of their toil, take part in the management of their shop, and so escape from their insecurity and dependence. It holds out the hope that in the socialist commonwealth they shall plant the vineyard and eat of the fruit thereof; they shall be full heirs of the science and art and education which they now labor to maintain, but into which, like Moses when he saw the Promised Land afar, they cannot enter.

Socialism always makes headway slowly at first. It requires hard thought. A man has to view all things from a new angle and revise all his maxims and value judgments. The leaders of the working class in any nation need a generation to assimilate it, and after that they have the task of popularizing it for the masses. But it never goes backward, and no industrial nation can escape its influence. It trusts more to intellectual conviction and less to emotion than any great movement of our day. Socialists appeal to the theoretical and historical intellect with almost wearisome exclusiveness. In Milwaukee nine-tenths of the party funds used to go for literature. The socialists are today the only preachers who love doctrinal preaching. Not since the days when Calvinism was convincing the intellect of northern Europe has any system of thought been expounded with such evangelistic zeal.

The fact is that socialism is the necessary spiritual product of capitalism. It has been formulated by that class which has borne the sins of capitalism in its own body and knows them by heart. It stands for the holy determination of that wronged and embittered class to eliminate those sins forever from the social life of mankind. Thus socialism is the historical nemesis of capitalism and follows it like its shadow. The only influence that can long seal the minds of the industrial working class against the doctrines of socialism is the power of religion in the hands of a strong Church. That influence has created solid organizations of nonsocialist workers in Europe. But socialism seeps in, even there. If those Catholic federations of workingmen which resist socialism in Germany were transferred bodily to America, their presence would be felt as a tremendous reinforcement of the socialist drift in our trades unionism. There is no way of taking the wind out of the sails of the socialist ship except to sail alongside of it and in the same direction. As a clever Irishman in Wisconsin puts it, "The only way to beat the socialists is to beat them to it." But when the enemies of a cause are compelled to aid it in order to oppose it, the stars in their courses are fighting against Sisera. The opponents of the Progressive party in 1912 called its platform socialism; Mr. Roosevelt called it a corrective of socialism; the *Boston Common* called it "an adaptation of the more imminent teachings of socialism for middle-class neophytes," and added, "Out from among the lowly and despised once more has come a message of guidance for humanity."

For the present argument the important fact is not the growing political power of the socialists, but the moral power of their cause. The Russian despotism also exerts vast political power, but that is in defiance of the conscience of mankind. Socialism appeals not only to the working class, but to the idealistic intellectuals. A great number of artists and literary men are socialists at large. Many of the magazine writers and political leaders to whom we owe much of the present awakening are near-socialists. The same thing is true of the teaching profession and of social workers. An eminent banker, a former Secretary of the Treasury, said in an address to college alumni as early as 1909:

I am alarmed at the trend toward socialism in this country today. If there is any power in this country to stem it, it ought to be the trained minds of college men. Four out of five commencement-day orations are purely socialistic. I have met many of the teachers of sociology in our schools and universities. With few exceptions these teachers are socialists, though they hesitate to admit it and most of them will deny it. Unconsciously there is a great deal of socialism being taught in these days from the pulpit. The Chautauqua is also full of it. I do not recall a Chautauqua popular speaker who is not talking and teaching socialist doctrines. The trend of the newspapers is towards socialism, and, I repeat, the trend is dangerous to this country.

Such a statement is correct only if we accept our definition of socialism from the timidity of a banker. But it is interesting to see this man call on the college men to come to the rescue, and yet confess that the college men have gone over to the enemy. But if in any great historic movement the men of property are on one side and the young and idealistic intellects are on the other, on which side is God?

The religious idealists constitute a special variety of the intellectual class. In their case, the power of religion is added as a potent ingredient to their higher life. No one can deny that the ethical life of our religious leaders is deeply tinged with a diluted socialism. Wherever a man has the prophetic cast of thought, the broader moral outlook, and the tongue of fire, we can discover clear affinity for socialist ideas. Those men who have kept their mental balance against the dogmatism of the cruder type of socialism, who have guarded the purity of their life against the looseness of modern morals, who have cherished the devoutness of intimate religion in the drought of skepticism, but who have also absorbed the socialist analysis of our collective sins and the socialist hope of a fraternal democracy, stand as a class marked by God as his own. The best of them belong to "that small transfigured band whom the world cannot tame."

Religious men are forced into a tragic dilemma when they face organized socialism. On the one hand they realize in its ideas the most thorough and consistent economic elaboration of the Christian social ideal. It is far and away the most powerful force for justice, democracy, and organized fraternity in the modern world. On the other hand, these moral elements are fused with an alloy that is repellent to their Christian instincts.

There are religious people who are not Christians. Their sympathies are not with the common people, but with the parasitic classes. They do not trust in freedom, but want a strong Church to lay down the law to the common man. If Jesus appeared in modern dress among such people, they would not know what to do with him. To such persons, of course, socialism is horrid. I am not concerned for them. I speak for men who have drawn their economic insight from socialism, and their democracy and moral ardor from Jesus himself, and who yet find it hard to co-operate wholeheartedly with party socialism as they actually find it.

When they attend socialist meetings, they encounter a rougher, directer, more dogmatic, more acrimonious tone of discussion than they are used to in gatherings of the educated classes. Also an entire absence of respect for many of their conventional objects of respect. But if they have the right stuff in them, they will get used to it and even come to like it as a proof of unvarnished sincerity and profound interest in the subject. But they will also find an almost universal attitude of suspicion and dislike against the Church, which often rises to downright hate and bitterness, and expands to general antagonism against religion itself. The materialistic philosophy of history as the average socialist expounds it, emphasizes the economic and material factors of life so exclusively that the spiritual elements of humanity seem as unimportant as the coloring of a flower or the bloom on the grape. In large parts of the party literature the social and economic teachings of socialism are woven through a web of materialistic philosophy, which is part of "scientific socialism." The party platform declares religion to be a private affair, but that declaration of neutrality does not exclude persistent attacks on religion by official exponents of the party. The practical deductions drawn from materialistic philosophy and from historical conceptions of the family, have combined with modern impatience of moral restraints to create in some of the intellectuals of the party loose views of sex life against which all the instincts of Christian training warn as poisonous.

If a Christian man sees the good in socialism and identifies himself with the organized movement, he is suspected of atheism, free love, and red-handed violence, and he cannot repudiate that charge against his party friends as mere slander. A man of mature religious convictions may discriminate between the economic doctrines of socialism, which are its essential, and the philosophical teachings, which are an adventitious historical taint of it. But others, who may be drawn into the party through his influence, may not be able to keep the two things apart.

Socialist leaders in America have committed an enormous tactical mistake in allowing socialism to be put in antagonism to Christianity. Why should they permit some of their agitators to go out of their way to belie the neutrality promised by the party platform? Why should they erect a barb-wire fence between the field of socialism and Christianity which makes it hard to pass from one to the other? Organized Christianity represents the largest fund of sobriety, moral health, good will, moral aspiration, teaching ability, and capacity to sacrifice for higher ends, which can be found in America. If Socialists will count up the writers, lecturers, and organizers who acquired their power of agitation and moral appeal through the training they got in church life, they will realize what an equipment for propaganda lies stored in the Christian churches. As soon as the Socialist party came to the point of being able to elect mayors and city officials, it found that Christian ministers somehow made up a large percentage of the men elected, which seems to argue that they have capacities that are not wholly contemptible. Many Socialist leaders misread the situation in America because they are obsessed by theories developed in Europe on the basis of the bad experience which democracy has had with the Roman Catholic Church and with the Protestant state churches. They know too little of religious history to be aware that religion is a very different thing in England and America where it has been loved and sustained for centuries by the free sacrifices of the plain people in their own little religious democracies. The autocratic churches of Europe have long done their best to suppress any spontaneous religious movements of the common man, and have succeeded very well in making personal religious experience almost unknown in large sections of the population. In England and America millions of the people have experienced the power of religion in their own lives, and when socialism undertakes to pull up Christianity, it will find it rooted deeper than in Europe. Surely socialism has its job cut out for it in overthrowing capitalism. Why should it force into the hostile camp the multitude of Christian men who are so close to it in their moral point of view? In England the best leaders of the Labor party are Christian men and active church workers. The leaders of German socialism are at a loss to understand a situation where Christian men can be also avowed Socialists. But that proves that the continental leaders are unfit to guide the policies of American socialism. If Socialist philosophy does not reckon with the actual facts of social life, it is not "scientific," but a stock of imported misinformation.

As long as socialism was an intense insistence on a few fundamental doctrines, and was upheld by a small body of minds bent on driving these doctrines home, it is comprehensible that the religious desires and emotions of the human soul were slighted or forgotten. But the more socialism aspires to become a rounded expression of all sound and wholesome human life, and the more it embodies the great masses of humanity, the more sectarian and narrow-minded will the traditional contempt for religion become. Jaurès, the brilliant French Socialist leader, heralds a broader view: "I believe it would be wearisome and even fatal to stifle the aspirations of the human conscience. I do not believe at all that the material and social life suffice for man. We want him to be able to rise to a religious conception of life by means of science, reason, and freedom. The hour has come for democracy no longer to mock or outrage the ancient faiths, but to seek whatever they contain that is living and true and can abide in an emancipated and broadened human conscience." [4]

The Socialists are not nearly as unbelieving as some of them try to make us believe. Their theories may make everything turn on "economic class interests"; they may scoff at moral ideals, and insist that it is all

[4] Paul Sabatier, in his *L'Orientation Religieuse de la France Actuelle* (p. 38), tells an interesting anecdote. At a great church festival in Lyon, at which all the bishops of southeastern France were present, the bishop who had preached the sermon was receiving the compliments of ladies and priests at a dinner. He told them he had just read one of the most beautiful sermons he had ever read in his life, and begged permission to read them extracts. When he finished, all demanded the name of the preacher. He asked them to guess. They ran through the list of the celebrated preachers of France, but in vain. At last he announced that it was an address by—Jaurès.

a "stomach question"; but they appeal to men to act contrary to their economic interests on behalf of humanity, and they themselves labor with a moral enthusiasm and a power of self-sacrifice which look most suspiciously like religion. "Nothing in the present day is so likely to awaken the conscience of the ordinary man or woman, or to increase the sense of individual responsibility, as a thorough course in socialism. The study of socialism has proved the turning point in thousands of lives, and converted self-seeking men and women into self-sacrificing toilers for the masses. The impartial observer can scarcely claim that the Bible produces so marked an effect upon the daily, habitual life of the average man and woman who profess to guide their conduct by it, as socialism does upon its adherents. The strength of socialism in this respect is more like that of early Christianity as described in the New Testament." [5] Jesus surprised the religious people of his day by telling them that the publicans and harlots had more religion than they. Between a church member who lifts no hand against commercial inhumanity because it would "hurt business," and an atheist who endangers his position and consumes his energies in fighting it, we might be in doubt who of the two really believes in God.

Time and experience will balance the philosophy of Socialism. No great mass movement in history was ever free from one-sidedness and error. When Christianity was pervading the pagan world of Rome, it feared and repudiated art, because art had grown up in the service of paganism and seemed inseparable from it. But in time the Church became the great patron of art. In the Reformation the Protestant minority was wrought to such a fighting pitch that it hated the entire Catholic Church as antichristian and devilish, and the Puritans cleared their churches of music and art because Catholicism had stamped them with its spirit. That dogmatic intolerance of a young movement fighting against the overwhelming pressure of an older social force is duplicated in socialism today. Religion bears the stamp of the older epoch in which it was developed, and socialism treats the Church as the Church treated pagan art and philosophy, and fears its gifts as Protestantism fears Catholicism. This seems intolerable, but it is human. While a movement is fluid and plastic, it takes the impress of its first environment and casts its doctrines and institutions in that mold. Jewish apocalypticism, Persian demonology, and Greek philosophy saturated early Christian thought and seemed part of the essence of Christianity to the early Church Fathers. Calvinism was molded by the stern, keen mind of John Calvin and by the civic institutions of Switzerland and proclaimed these equipments as part of the eternal gospel. Compared with

[5] R. T. Ely, *Socialism and Social Reform*, 145.

the tenacity with which religion clings to its early prejudices or superstitions, socialism has shown a very sweet reasonableness in the speed with which it has left some things behind.

To me the greatest danger seems to lie in the loss of that teachableness. When I try to look at socialism as coming centuries may look back at it, I fear the solidity of the Socialist parties and the intensity of their party spirit. An organization created for fighting purposes does not melt away when the fighting is done, but its maintenance becomes an end in itself and therewith the organization becomes a drag on social progress. The history of the Republican party and the useless perpetuation of many of our religious sects prove that. Pure love of the truth and independent thought do not flourish in the midst of party spirit. The internal history of socialism shows how quickly a narrow and jealous orthodoxy springs up within the party and forbids the prompt assimilation of larger knowledge. Important sections of the party fear "the intellectuals," just as religious sects have feared their educated men. I realize that socialism needs a steel edge to cut through the obstacles that confront it, and only party loyalty, party dogmatism, and even party hatred can temper that edge, but I wish the coming generations could be spared what we are preparing for them. Whoever solidifies the opposition to socialism, inevitably solidifies Socialist party spirit, and when it is a Church that does it, it solidifies Socialist irreligion. The Roman Catholic Church laments and despises the sectarian divisions of Protestantism, but it is itself chiefly responsible for them. Its arrogance, its egotism, its refusal to be reformed by anything except the sledge-hammer blows of the Almighty's chastisement, necessitated the agonies that bled Christendom white and consolidated the reforming elements into fighting bodies which still perpetuate the dead issues of that fight after four centuries. Socialism inevitably involves a menace. It is our business to make its menace small and its blessing great.

Aside from the dangers involved in party orthodoxy we may safely trust that socialism will slough off its objectionable elements as it matures. Those qualities against which the spirit of genuine Christianity justly protests are not of the essence of socialism. The loose views of marriage in some individuals are largely a bacterial contagion contracted from the outside. The materialism of the Socialist philosophy of history is the result of throwing a great truth out of balance; Christian doctrine, too, has often been one-sided by overemphasis of some truth. Atheism is in no way essential to Socialist thought. Socialists have no monopoly of it. It was the popular philosophy of continental liberalism in the '50's and '60's, and the leaders of the working class absorbed it as true "science." Christianity was the religion of the possessing classes and was used as a spiritual force to hold down socialism; consequently revolutionary thought seized the philosophy that seemed most effectively to maul Christianity.[6] The Socialists found the Church against them, and thought God was against them too. They have had to do God's work without the sense of God's presence to hearten them. When a great moral movement has been infected with dogmatic unbelief, partly through the sin of the European churches, shall we back away from it in fear, or have we confidence enough in our own religion to take part in it? Can we prove in our own personality that the highest type of socialism is that which combines the economic intelligence and political force of socialism with the character and faith created by religion?

Whatever the sins of individual Socialists, and whatever the short-comings of Socialist organizations, they are tools in the hands of the Almighty. They must serve him whether they will or not. "He maketh the wrath of man to praise him, and the remainder of wrath he turneth aside." Whatever tares grow in the field of socialism the field was plowed and sown by the Lord, and he will reap it. Socialism is one of the chief powers of the coming age. Its fundamental aims are righteous, not because they are socialistic, but because they are human. They were part of the mission of Christianity before the name of socialism had been spoken. God had to raise up socialism because the organized Church was too blind, or too slow, to realize God's ends. The Socialist parties, their technical terms, and their fighting dogmas will pass away into ancient history when their work is done. The only thing that will

[6] Professor Werner Sombart, *Sozialismus und soziale Bewegung*, p. 91, thinks the hostility of the proletarian movement against religion has a theoretical and a practical cause. The theoretical cause is that socialism in its youth absorbed the bald atheism which was the philosophy of the semi-educated classes in the middle of the nineteenth century. This dogmatic atheism is now definitely outgrown by science. "No serious representative of science will today dare to assert that science demands atheism or excludes religion." Therefore the proletariat would now be free to come out of the atheistic dogmatism into which it backed up. But practical causes still keep it there. The enthusiasm for unbelief was caused by the feeling that the philosophy of materialism was a mighty revolutionary explosive, fit to break the hold of the existing authorities. It opposed the Christian philosophy of the ruling classes. "For no one ought to be in doubt that in the great majority of cases official Christianity was utilized by the ruling classes against the proletarian movement for greater liberty. The fate inflicted on dissenting Christians is the best proof for that. As long as monarchy and capitalism are defended as divine institutions, every social movement of our day had to turn against the church and against religion." He adds that these causes will disappear as soon as Christianity takes a neutral position, or becomes friendly to socialism.

last and the only thing that matters is the Reign of God in humanity, and the Reign of God is vaster and higher than socialism. The great danger is that our eyes will be blinded by ecclesiastical prejudices so that we do not know God when he comes close to us. The Jewish Church had the sacred book and the heritage of the prophets. Yet when He came who fulfilled the law and the prophets, they turned against him. He was identified with publicans and sinners, and he seemed to overthrow morality and religion.

*

THE REVIVAL OF RELIGION AND THE CONVERSION OF THE STRONG

IN LOOKING back over the field traversed in this book, it may seem to some as if our argument had fallen away from the high religious ground taken at the outset and had sagged down to the level of mere economic discussion. That impression would be superficial. This is a religious book from beginning to end. Its sole concern is for the Kingdom of God and the salvation of men. But the Kingdom of God includes the economic life; for it means the progressive transformation of all human affairs by the thought and spirit of Christ. And a full salvation also includes the economic life; for it involves the opportunity for every man to realize the full humanity which God has put into him as a promise and a call; it means a clean, rich, just, and brotherly life between him and his fellows; it means a chance to be singlehearted, and not to be coerced into a double life. I believe with the great historian Von Ranke that "the only real progress of mankind is contained in Christianity"; but that is true only when Christianity is allowed to become "the internal, organizing force of society." [1] We have scouted around our economic system, mined under it, and airplaned over it, because this is the fortress in which the predatory and unbrotherly spirit still lies entrenched with flags flying. It is the strategical key to the spiritual conquest of the modern world.

But, on the other hand, no outward economic readjustments will answer our needs. It is not this thing or that thing our nation needs, but a new mind and heart, a new conception of the way we all ought to live together, a new conviction about the worth of a human life and the use God wants us to make of our own lives. We want a revolution both inside and outside. We want a moral renovation of public opinion

[1] Fichte.

and a revival of religion. Laws and constitutions are mighty and search-ing, but while the clumsy hand of the law fumbles at the gate below, the human soul sits in its turret amid its cruel plunder and chuckles. A righteous public opinion may bring the proudest sinner low. But the most pervasive scrutiny, a control which follows our actions to their fountainhead where the desires and motives of the soul are born, is exerted only by personal religion.

But here again we are compelled to turn to our economic life. What if the public opinion on which we rely is tainted and purposely poi-soned? What if our religion is drugged and sick? The mammonism generated by our economic life is debilitating our religion so that its hand lies nerveless on our conscience. Jesus told us it would be so. He put the dilemma flatly before us: "Ye cannot serve God and Mammon. If ye love the one, ye will hate the other." Every proof that we love Mammon with all our heart and all our soul raises the presumption that we have lost the love of God and are merely going through the motions when we worship him. We can measure the general apostasy by noting the wonder and love that follow every man who has even in some slight degree really turned his back on money. Men crowd around him like exiles around a man who brings them news from home.

So we must begin at both ends simultaneously. We must change our economic system in order to preserve our conscience and our religious faith; we must renew and strengthen our religion in order to be able to change our economic system. This is a two-handed job; a one-handed man will bungle it. I have discussed the economic system in many chap-ters. In this closing chapter I shall talk about revolutionary religion and the need of converted men for the christianizing of the social order.

When Archimedes discovered the laws of leverage, he cried Δὸς ποῦ στῶ. He thought he could hoist the bulk of the earth from its grooves if only he had a standing place and a fulcrum for his lever. God wants to turn humanity right side up, but he needs a fulcrum. Every saved soul is a fixed point on which God can rest his lever. A divine world is ever pressing into this imperfect and sinful world, demanding admission and realization for its higher principles, and every inspired man is a channel through which the spirit of God can enter humanity. Every higher era must be built on a higher moral law and a purer experience of religion. Therefore the most immediate and constant need in chris-tianizing the social order is for more religious individuals.

I believe in the miraculous power of the human personality. A mind set free by God and energized by a great purpose is an incomputable force. Lord Shaftesbury was naturally a man of rather narrow type and without brilliant gifts, but he gave himself with religious devotion to the cause of the oppressed classes, and so became one of the prime forces that swung England out of its carnival of capitalistic inhumanity.[2] If we in the West have been correctly informed, the emancipation of China from the Manchu oligarchy has been chiefly due to the personal teaching and persuasion of one man, Sun Yat Sen, and the band of devoted men whom he raised up. One of the most fruitful intellectual movements in Germany [3] owes its beginning to one man, Professor Albert Eichhorn. His health has been so frail that he has published nothing but a sixteen-page pamphlet, but by personal conversations he inspired a number of able young minds, setting them new problems and fertilizing their thinking by his unselfish co-operation. The Democratic Convention of Baltimore in 1912 will stand out in our memory chiefly for the dramatic power of a single personality, strong in his sincerity and the trust of his countrymen, to wrest the control of his party at least for a time from evil hands. The history of the new democracy in recent years is the history of small groups of men of conviction and courage who stood together for the new democratic measures. Often without official standing or financial backing they have shattered political redoubts that seemed impregnable. The Inquisition of the Middle Ages and the Siberian exile system alike testify to the fact that the powers of tyranny are afraid of single-handed faith.

This power of the individual rests on the social cohesion of mankind. Because we are bound together in unity of life, the good or the evil in one man's soul affects the rest. The presence of one heart that loves humanity shames the selfish spirit in others and warms the germs of civic devotion in the chilly soil, so that they grow and bear seed in turn. One brave soul rallies the timid and shakes the self-confidence of the prosperous. One far-seeing man can wake the torpid imagination of a community so that men see civic centers where they saw only real estate deals before. Hopes and convictions that were dim and vague become concrete, beautiful, and compelling when they take shape in a life that lives them out. No torch is kindled of itself, but when one man has lighted his at the altar fire of God, hundreds will take their light from him. So the faith of the pioneers becomes socialized. The belief of the few in time becomes a dogma which does not have to be proved over and over, but is a spiritual fund owned in common by a great social group. We need new dogmas that will raise the old to a

[2] The Duke of Argyll in 1885 said: "My Lords, the social reforms of the last century have not been mainly due to the Liberal Party. They have been due mainly to the influence, character, and perseverance of one man, Lord Shaftesbury." "That," said Lord Salisbury, "is, I believe, a very true representation of the facts."

[3] The so-called *religionsgeschichtliche Schule.*

new level and give them wider scope. "You have heard that it was said of old time—But I say unto you." [4] Such a lifting of moral conviction comes through those who can speak with authority because they speak for God.

Create a ganglion chain of redeemed personalities in a commonwealth, and all things become possible. "What the soul is in the body, that are Christians in the world." [5] The political events of 1912 have furnished fresh proof that after individuals have preached their faith long enough, the common mind reaches the point of saturation, and moral conviction begins to be precipitated in solid layers. At such times even poor Judas thinks he would like to join the Messianic movement and be an apostle, and the rotten nobility of France follow the peasant girl:

The White Maid, and the white horse, and the flapping banner of God;
Black hearts riding for money; red hearts riding for fame;
The Maid who rides for France, and the king who rides for shame;
Gentlemen, fools, and a saint riding in Christ's high name. [6]

"Force and Right rule the world; Force till Right is ready." [7] The more individuals we have who love the Right for its own sake and move toward it of their own will, the less force and compulsion do we need. Here is one of the permanent functions of the Christian Church. It must enlist the will and the love of men and women for God, mark them with the cross of Christ, and send them out to finish up the work which Christ began. Is the Church supplying society with the necessary equipment of such personalities? Let us grant that it can never reach all; but is it making Christian revolutionists of those whom it does teach and control? Jesus feared the proselyting efforts of the Jewish Church, because it made men worse than they were before. [8] Some people today who carry the stamp of ecclesiastical religion most legibly are the most hopeless cases so far as social spirit and effort are concerned. The spiritual efficiency of the Church is therefore one of the most serious practical questions for the christianizing of the social order. We have shown [9] that the American churches have been to a large extent christianized in their fundamental organization, and every step in their redemption has facilitated social progress and increased the

[4] Matt. 5.
[5] The Epistle to Diognetus, chap. VI. Probably of the second century.
[6] Theodore Roberts, "The Maid."
[7] Rochefoucauld.
[8] Matt. xxiii. 15.
[9] Pt. III, chap. II.

forces available for righteousness. But the process of christianizing the Church is not yet complete.

To become fully Christian the churches must turn their back on dead issues and face their present tasks. There is probably not a single denomination which is not thrusting on its people questions for which no man would care and of which only antiquarians would know if the churches did not keep these questions alive. Our children sometimes pull the clothes of their grandparents out of old chests in the attic and masquerade in long-tailed coats and crinolines. We religious folks who air the issues of the sixteenth century go through the same mummery in solemn earnest, while the enemy is at the gate.

To become fully Christian and to do their duty by society the churches must get together. The disunion of the Church wastes the funds intrusted to it, wastes the abilities of its servants, and wastes the power of religious enthusiasm or turns it into antisocial directions. Civil war is always bad; it is worst when a nation is threatened by outside enemies and the very existence of the fatherland is in danger. Some churches are so far apart on essential matters that union is hopeless for the present. But the great body of Protestant Christians in America is simply perpetuating trivial dissensions in which scarcely any present-day religious values are at stake.

To become fully Christian the Church must come out of its spiritual isolation. In theory and practice the Church has long constituted a world by itself. It has been governed by ecclesiastical motives and interests which are often remote from the real interests of humanity, and has almost uniformly set church questions ahead of social questions. It has often built a sound-proof habitation in which people could live for years without becoming definitely conscious of the existence of prostitution, child labor, or tenement crowding. It has offered peace and spiritual tranquillity to men and women who needed thunderclaps and lightnings. Like all the rest of us, the Church will get salvation by finding the purpose of its existence outside of itself, in the Kingdom of God, the perfect life of the race.

To become fully Christian the Church must still further emancipate itself from the dominating forces of the present era. In an age of political despotism our fathers cut the Church loose from state control and state support, and therewith released the moral forces of progress. In an age of financial autocracy we must be far more watchful than we have been lest we bargain away the spiritual freedom of the Church for opulent support.

We do not want to substitute social activities for religion. If the Church comes to lean on social preachings and doings as a crutch because its religion has become paralytic, may the Lord have mercy on us all! We do not want less religion; we want more; but it must be a religion that gets its orientation from the Kingdom of God. To concentrate our efforts on personal salvation, as orthodoxy has done, or on soul culture, as liberalism has done, comes close to refined selfishness. All of us who have been trained in egotistic religion need a conversion to Christian Christianity, even if we are bishops or theological professors. Seek ye first the Kingdom of God and God's righteousness, and the salvation of your souls will be added to you. Our personality is of divine and eternal value, but we see it aright only when we see it as part of mankind. Our religious individuality must get its interpretation from the supreme fact of social solidarity. "What hast thou that thou hast not received?" Then what hast thou that thou dost not owe? Prayer ought to be a keen realization of our fellows, and not a forgetfulness of the world. A religion which realizes in God the bond that binds all men together can create the men who will knit the social order together as an organized brotherhood.

This, then, is one of the most practical means for the christianizing of the social order, to multiply the number of minds who have turned in conscious repentance from the old maxims, the old admirations, and the old desires, and have accepted for good and all the Christian law with all that it implies for modern conditions. When we have a sufficient body of such, the old order will collapse like the walls of Jericho when the people "shouted with a great shout" and "every man went straight before him" at the wall. No wrong can stand very long after the people have lost their reverence for it and begin to say "Booh" to it.

Mending the social order is not like repairing a clock in which one or two parts are broken. It is rather like restoring diseased or wasted tissues, and when that has to be done, every organ and cell of the body is heavily taxed. During the reconstructive process every one of us must be an especially good cell in whatever organ of the social body we happen to be located. The tissues of society which it will be hardest to replace by sound growth are represented by the class of the poor and the class of the rich. Both are the product of ages of social disease. Christianizing the social order involves a sanitation of the defective and delinquent classes, and of the classes living on unearned incomes. All these need religious salvation.

Suppose that we had successfully democratized our government, made our laws just, and socialized our industries. We should still have with us a great body of people who have been crippled by war or industry, exhausted by child labor, drained of vitality in their mothers' wombs, unbalanced by alcoholism, or made neurotic by drug habits and sexual excesses. These would be the legacy bequeathed by the old order to the new, and surviving it for at least fifty years; perhaps a hundred and fifty years. Today we have that same body of defective people, constantly replenished and increasing in proportion to the population, hanging as a dead weight on society and on the working class especially. Whatever decreases that weight will give us elbow room for constructive work. The men and women who are helping to organize the defective members of the community so that they will get the maximum enjoyment out of their life and will present the minimum of hindrance to the present social transition, are not mere ministers of mercy, but constructive agents in the christianizing of the social order. If the selfish political henchmen who have run our public institutions can be replaced by regenerate intellects, our institutions of mercy will come out of their conspiracy of silence with the workers of cruelty, and we shall begin to find out who and what is throwing all this burden on the community.

The problem of healing the social tissues is even more difficult in the case of those who break the laws. The old vindictive method of punishment has manifestly been ineffective. It is also unchristian; for nothing is Christian that is not impelled by love and the desire to redeem. It becomes increasingly intolerable as our clearer psychological knowledge reminds us that we all in youth had the same wayward and brutal instincts, and that the majority of youthful criminals are just such immature human beings as our own children. We are realizing that the social disorder which we ourselves have helped to create is responsible for a large part of our lawlessness. "Society stands in the docket with every criminal who is there." [10] We need redeemed minds to deal with the delinquents of society. The men and women who deal with offenders should be the wisest and most Christlike persons in the community. To save the young and wayward from losing their honor and to fan the dying fire of manhood in older criminals, is a great ministry of Christ, and Christian men ought to enter the police force with the sense of enlisting for God and their country. Within this generation our prisons should become redemptive institutions. But the consciousness of doing productive and honorable work is an essential condition of true salvation. Our penal institutions must become co-operative industrial establishments, where offenders can still support their families, lay by for the day when they will be thrown on their own resources, and, if possible, make restitution to those whom they have harmed. Our prisons must cease to be slave pens where the state lends its physical compulsion to some predatory industrial concern that wants

[10] Victor Hugo.

to make big profits by underselling outside labor, grafting on the state, and draining the prisoners. The participation of our states in contract prison labor is an indefensible business that ought to rob us of our sleep.

The sanitation of the wealthy classes is another problem; there we deal, not with the misery and waywardness of the poor, but with excessive material power. Some think it is idle to appeal to the rich to change their own lives; it will have to be changed for them. I do not believe it. As a class they will doubtless go their way, eating and drinking, marrying and giving in marriage till the flood comes. But individuals will respond; more of them, I believe, than in any similar situation in history before. Large groups of them have of late traveled miles in the direction of the fraternal life.

Even if there are only a few, their coming counts. Something happens when Moses leaves the palace of Pharaoh and joins the fortunes of his people. At a directors' meeting a single steady voice lifted for humanity and 6 per cent and against inhumanity and 8 per cent, cannot be disregarded forever, and that voice may mean health and decency for hundreds. Socialists justly say that there is no instance in history where one of the possessing classes has voluntarily given up its privileges. But is there any case where a poor and oppressed class has made a permanent and successful advance toward emancipation without help from individuals of the higher classes?

The desire for social esteem is one of the strongest and most subtle forces in social life. The individual always toils for whatever his class regards as the game. He will collect scalps for his belt, Philistine foreskins for a bridal gift to his beloved, silver cups or wreaths of wild olive as athletic trophies, funny titles, shady millions—it's all the same thing. Now, a few self-confident men can create a new basis of esteem in their class and therewith change the direction of effort. If a few redeemed minds in a given business community begin to yawn at the stale game of piling up and juggling money, and plunge into the more fascinating game of remaking a city, others will follow them. They cannot help it. God and the instinct of imitation will make them.

Social institutions can be hit hardest by men who have grown up inside of them and know their weak spots. Pharisaism was hit by the Pharisee Paul; monasticism by the monk Luther; the aristocracy of France by Count Mirabeau; alcoholism by John B. Gough; militarism by the ex-officer Tolstoy; frenzied finance by Lawson; the traction system by the traction magnate Tom L. Johnson. Even a few renegades from the rich are invaluable. It takes a sharp blow from the outside to crack an eggshell; the soft bill of a chick can break it from within.

Every rich man who has taken the Christian doctrine of stewardship seriously has thereby expropriated himself after a fashion and become manager where he used to be owner. If a man in addition realizes that some part of his fortune consists of unearned money, accumulated by one of the forms of injustice which have been legalized by our social order, it becomes his business as a Christian and a gentleman to make restitution in some way. There is no sincere repentance without restitution and confession of wrong. If I discovered that I or my grandfather had, knowingly or unknowingly, by some manipulation or error of the survey, added to my farm a ten-acre strip which belonged to my neighbor, could I go on harvesting the crops on it and say nothing? It is true that restitution of wealth absorbed from great communities through many years is a complicated matter, and that the giving away of large sums is dangerous business which may do as much harm as good. Yet some way must be found. Since the rich have gained their wealth by appropriating public functions and by using the taxing powers which ought to belong to the community alone, the fittest way of restitution is to undertake public service for which the state in its present impoverished condition has no means, such as the erection and running of public baths, playgrounds, and civic centers. But the moral value of such gifts would be almost incalculably increased if some acknowledgment were made that these funds were drawn from the people and belonged to them. Every time any rich man has indicated that he felt troubled in mind about his right to his wealth, the public heart has warmed toward him with a sense of forgiveness. If some eminent man should have the grace and wisdom to make a confession of wrong on behalf of his whole class, it would have a profound influence on public morality and social peace.

If a rich man has a really redeemed conscience and intellect, the best way to give away his unearned wealth would be to keep it and use it as a tool to make the recurrence of such fortunes as his own forever impossible. The Salvation Army sets a saved girl to save other girls, and that is the best way to keep her saved. By the same token a man whose forefathers made their money in breweries or distilleries ought to use it to fight alcoholism; a man who made his by land speculation should help to solve the housing question or finance the single-tax movement; a man who has charged monopoly prices for the necessaries of life should teach the people to organize co-operative societies; and so forth.

Men and women of the wealthy class who have been converted to the people as well as to God can perform a service of the highest value by weakening the resistance which their classes will inevitably offer to the equalization of property. That resistance has been by far the most important cause why humanity has been so backward in its social and moral development. The resistance of the upper classes has again and again blocked and frustrated hopeful upward movements, kept useful classes of the people in poverty and degradation, and punished the lovers of humanity with martyrdom of body or soul. The cross of Christ stands for the permanent historical fact that the men who have embodied the saving power of God have always been ill treated by those who profited by sin. Reference has been made to the work of Lord Shaftesbury.[11] In Lancashire alone he found 35,000 children under thirteen years of age, many of them only five or six years old, working fourteen and fifteen hours a day. It took Shaftesbury and his friends fourteen years of agitation to get a ten-hour bill passed, and even then it was so impeded by legal difficulties that successive Acts, chiefly instigated by him, were required to give it effect, and the ten-hour standard was not fully secured till 1874. He and his friends were loaded with denunciation and insult for years. Few clergymen stood by him; they were indifferent, or cowed by the cotton lords. Men whose names are revered because they led the fight of the capitalistic class against landed wealth, Cobden, Bright, and Gladstone, were at that time malignant opponents of the protection of the working class. Machiavelli said that men will forgive the murder of their parents more easily than the spoliation of their property.

Of course the road is smoother since democracy has leveled it. In 1567 under the Duke of Alba a man was condemned to death for the treasonable assertion that "we must obey God rather than man." It would probably be safe to say that now, especially if chapter and verse were quoted. But the opposition of the powerful classes against every movement that seriously threatens their privileges is one of the most formidable facts with which we have to reckon. All the dynasties of Europe combined against the first French Republic. All capitalistic governments would combine to trip and cripple the first Socialist Republic. If our Interests found their control of government really in danger, it would be comparatively easy to embroil our nation in war; that is always the last trick of a tottering dynasty. Therewith the President would be vested with almost dictatorial powers; martial law could be proclaimed wherever needed; State rights could be overridden; and the popular movement could be forcibly suppressed as treasonable.

A minority of wealthy men and women, who stand for the democratic American ideals and sincerely believe in the necessity and justice of the impending social changes, would do a great deal to avert the head-

[11] Hodder, *The Life and Work of the Seventh Earl of Shaftesbury*, 3 vols., 1886.

ing up of that spirit of anarchy among the rich and to prevent such a coup d'état, which would be the beginning of the end for our nation.

But the call is to all. "The Kingdom of God is at hand. Therefore repent and believe in the Gospel." I wish the Student Volunteers could add another pledge by which those who do not go to the foreign field would bind themselves to give some term of their youth at least to social work in the trenches. If necessary, young men and women should be willing to secure their freedom for poorly paid work by postponing marriage. Childless men and women are under a special law to make good to the race what they are not putting into the bearing and rearing of children. Those whose love has suffered a great loss should fill the gap with a wider love, and do for humanity what their loved one would have been worth to his fellow men if he had lived. Those who have suffered through some social sin can give a meaning and value to their suffering by making it serve the redemption of the race from that sin. For instance, if a man has borne the curse of alcohol or drug poison in himself or in the degradation of a friend, he is under holy bonds to warn others and stamp out that evil; if a woman has felt sex sin cutting into her heart or her body, she has a special call from God to save humanity from that silent ravager, and if she is deaf to the call, her suffering, in place of being part of God's salvation, becomes a mere waste and loss. On the ancient minster at Basle are two sculptured groups: St. Martin cutting his cloak in two with his sword to clothe a beggar, and St. George spurring his horse against the dragon that devastated the country. Every Christian man should embody both kinds of sainthood in one life.

> Trumpeter, sound for the splendor of God!
> Sound the music whose name is law,
> Whose service is perfect freedom still,
> The order august that rules the stars!
> Bid the anarchs of night withdraw.
> Too long the destroyers have worked their will.
> Sound for the last, the last of the wars!
> Sound for the heights that our fathers trod,
> When truth was truth and love was love,
> With a hell beneath, but a heaven above.
> Trumpeter, rally us, rally us, rally us,
>   On to the City of God.

* IV *

A Social Litany

*I*N 1913 the parcel post system went into operation, the income tax
amendment to the Constitution became effective, and the Federal
Reserve System was established. President Wilson said in a speech at
Chicago that monopolies must end.

Ty Cobb was a popular baseball player, as interest in professional
baseball spread. The public was also fascinated by new mechanical
achievements in aviation. More and more movie houses opened.

Among books widely discussed was Winston Churchill's The Inside
of the Cup, in which the American novelist considered the dilemmas
of an urban clergyman who declared himself on social issues and in-
curred opposition within his own congregation. Other books with wide
circulation included: A Personal Narrative of Political Experience by
Robert M. La Follette; The Business of Being a Woman by Ida Tarbell;
Roast Beef Medium by Edna Ferber; The Woman Thou Gavest Me
by Hall Caine; The Dark Flower by John Galsworthy; The Interpretation of Dreams by Sigmund Freud.

Protestant denominations continued to pronounce on social questions. The Federal Council of the Churches of Christ in America, organized in 1908, was now growing and becoming more active as a
co-operative agency of the middle-of-the-road Protestant denominations.
The Council carried on various tasks which these religious bodies
thought best to be carried out in common, including conventional
evangelistic programs and the somewhat newer interests of social service and international justice and good will. Social service secretaries of
the several denominations came together for co-operative planning under the Council's auspices, evidencing marked interest in labor's right
to organize and in backing social legislation, such as the regulation of
child labor.

Local churches, or at least a minority of them, showed a budding
interest in the national social pronouncements. "Labor Sunday" was
promoted, on the Sunday before the national holiday. Labor Sunday

messages were read in some local churches. The sympathy expressed with the aspirations of organized labor brought consternation in a portion of the bench-warmers' ranks. There were signs of a ferment of social discussion in various church quarters. Urban churches began to plan diversification of their staffs as they thought of broadening their social services to their members. More and more pastors thought it would be good to encourage social legislation.

Rauschenbusch had boldly recommended a sort of alliance between the churches and the rising labor movement, so as to achieve an effective social reconstruction. Among his writing published in 1913 was a litany.

The quotation that follows, "A Social Litany," was used at a mass meeting under the auspices of the Joint Commission on Social Service held at the General Convention of the Protestant Episcopal Church, New York, 1913.

Rauschenbusch's prayers, selections quoted below, are categorized as the nonliturgical type. The production of new materials for liturgical use is a most difficult art. Rauschenbusch, the Baptist, was, as has been noted earlier, highly critical of traditional liturgy because he believed that it was only nurturing individualism in religion. He was, of course, as critical of conventional church services in the evangelical churches of which he was a part, and for the same reason.

Undoubtedly, personal prayer was the main wellspring of this mystic and prophet. But to him there were always three forces involved: God, the self-praying, and fellow men. He was always most appreciative of the worshiping congregation, and his total plea was for a more effective corporate witness along with a personal one. The child of God praying could not complete the act of worship without duty to others of the human family.

This great conviction is expressed in the litany that follows.

※

FROM the sins that divide us, from all class bitterness and race hatred, from forgetfulness of thee and indifference to our fellowmen:

Good Lord, deliver us.

From the corruption of the franchise and of civil government, from greed and from the arbitrary love of power:

Good Lord, deliver us.

From the fear of unemployment and the evils of overwork, from the curse of child-labor and the ill-paid toil of women:
> Good Lord, deliver us.

From the luxury that enervates, from the poverty that stultifies:
> Good Lord, deliver us.

That it may please thee to unite the inhabitants of every city, state and nation in the bonds of peace and concord:
> We beseech thee to hear us, Good Lord.

That thy followers may be strong to achieve industrial justice, and to bid the oppressed go free:
> We beseech thee to hear us, Good Lord.

That the labor movement may be confirmed in disinterested honor, and that the employers of labor may fashion their dealings according to the laws of equity:
> We beseech thee to hear us, Good Lord.

That thou wilt help us to give all men health of body and soul:
> We beseech thee to hear us, Good Lord.

That the watchword of the Christian state, "Thou shalt love thy neighbor as thyself," may become a command with power:
> We beseech thee to hear us, Good Lord.

That the spirit of reconciliation may be made manifest among men:
> We beseech thee to hear us, Good Lord.

That it may please thee to inspire thy Church with the vision of the New Jerusalem coming down from heaven to men, and that thy Kingdom may come on earth:
> We beseech thee to hear us, Good Lord.

The grace of our Lord Jesus Christ, and the love of God, and the fellowship of the Holy Spirit be with us all evermore. Amen.[1]

---

[1] First Published by *The Survey*.

* V *

Dare We Be Christians?

*I*N 1914 Henry Ford announced that every worker over twenty-two years of age in the Ford Motor Company would be paid a minimum of five dollars a day. Mr. Ford observed that the rewards from industry had gone more heavily to capital than to labor, and said that labor was entitled to a greater share. The effect on the American public was electric.

General Coxey marched on Washington again with numbers of the unemployed. He attracted less attention than in 1894. Newspaper editorials expressed anger at jobless who engaged in public demonstrations.

The Federal Trade Commission was established as an agency to aid in enforcement of the antitrust laws.

The first radio broadcast was made. Stations in the Wanamaker stores of New York and Philadelphia enabled employees to speak from city to city. Music was also broadcast.

World War I began. Andrew Carnegie gave two million dollars to the Church Peace Union, which sought international conciliation through the churches. Mother's Day was established by presidential proclamation. Churches immediately paid attention to it, to the delight of the florists.

Among popular books, Penrod by Booth Tarkington "went like wildfire." It was all about one boy's exploits. Others were Neighborhood Stories by Zona Gale; Mothers and Children by Dorothy Canfield; Cap'n Dan's Daughter by Joseph C. Lincoln.

Among churches a revival of sorts in interest in social issues was established. The hopes for a peace to last a thousand years were rudely shattered by European events. The public, including the church public, began to follow the war news. Rauschenbusch and a contingent of followers—or persons with like interests—were in demand as speakers. The churches continued to pronounce on social issues and began to collect money for the relief of war victims.

A brief but trenchant offering from the prophet's pen was a booklet,

Dare We Be Christians? *It was first published in Boston by Pilgrim Press in 1914. By that time Rauschenbusch had already published three of his major works in English—Christianity and the Social Crisis, Christianizing the Social Order, and Prayers of the Social Awakening. Ray Stannard Baker had interviewed Rauschenbusch and on the basis of the conversations had written an article,* "The Spiritual Unrest, a Vision of the New Christianity," *published in the American Magazine.*

Men and women of all sorts and conditions were going to the storehouse and the powerhouse in Rauschenbusch's mind. But particularly was this true of persons who were active in social and political organizations and in the agencies that influenced public opinion. Theologians, ministers, and missionaries consulted him.

The introduction to Dare We Be Christians? *opens with* "Paul's Praise of Love." *There is an exposition of Chapter 13 of I Corinthians.* "Have we faith enough to believe that the Christian doctrine of love is the solution of our big modern questions?" *There was need of an interpretation of the great biblical teaching. Then Rauschenbusch presented his own, as follows.*

*

W^E NEED a modern supplement to Paul's praise of love, written in the face of present-day problems and with a twentieth-century point of view, but with the same old Christian enthusiasm for love and the same old faith in the power of Jesus Christ to inspire love. I have not Paul's mind. I have neither the severe consistency of his reasoning nor the swift terseness of his phrases nor the blazing heat of his sacrificial enthusiasm—and it seems an amusing work of supererogation even to disavow any such thought. But I take him at his word—that "there are diversities of gifts but the same spirit"—and propose to write a few variations on his *leitmotif*, which he, in turn, got from our common Master.

The Scope of Love in Society

In order to understand the place of love in human life we must first understand the scope of the word we use, the manifoldness and reach of the force we are to discuss.

Whenever the Christian religion comes to a new people, it finds the native vocabulary defective for its special purposes. In the rich vocabulary of the Greek language it could find plenty of words to express hate, but none that signified humility without casting on it the slur of servility, and none that signified love without a taint of sexual suggestiveness. When the King James' Version was made for the English the translators of this chapter took refuge in the frosty word "charity" as more ecclesiastical, safe, and proper. The men who made the Revised Version in 1881 risked the plain English "love," but even yet the idea of sex dominates the involuntary associations of ideas which it drags along with it.

The attraction between man and woman is indeed the most striking and stirring form of love. We can gauge its force by the intense joy of its satisfactions, and the agony when love is unrequited or its trust wronged or its faithfulness broken. Two persons, at opposite poles in their physical tastes, their aesthetic habits, their aims in life, perhaps strangers to each other until recently, break away from the family bonds of a lifetime and enter into a physical and mental intimacy of life which binds them in a lasting social partnership of work and mutual care. If it were not an old story it would be a miracle. Even its reflected sensations are so charming that we never tire of reading love stories or discreetly watching them in real life.

But the love of the sexes is only a specialized form of that larger love which pervades our race. The absorbing interest that lovers take in each other is only an enrichment and intensification of that purely human interest which we take in any person we like. The more of that general interest there is fused with the special passion, the nobler and more durable will it be. If there is nothing but sex desire we call it vice. As Tolstoy has finely said, a man loves his wife purely if he thinks of her as his sister as well as his wife.

The institution of the family places upon sex love a heavy load of work and obligation, and so tames it. Society practically says to sex desire what Paul said to emotional religion: "Thou must be socially useful or thou shalt get no respect or countenance from us. If thou wilt form a co-operative group for service and bear children for humanity, we will honor and protect; if not, we will punish." There are some who think it would be wiser to take the saddle, the bit and the bridle from this vagrant and restless and greedy desire, letting it bear only such social obligations as it chooses and as long as it chooses. I do not care to live long enough to see that.

Through the attraction of man and maid love is always weaving new combinations of lives, reaching out to the right and to the left and knitting threads that had no connections before, bringing whole groups of families into friendly co-operation and laughing at the efforts of the proud to isolate themselves from the rest of their kind.

At the same time love is preparing to connect the present and the future generations. To lovers their love seems their own peculiar joy and apart from all the world. But humanity stands in the shadow behind them and lifts the majestic hands of blessing above them. The indomitable spirit of the race is reaching out in them toward the better days that are to be and is flinging a new defiance to death as they affirm life together.

Out of their union buds the next generation of men, and at once love springs forward to bind the young and the mature in a new and amazing bond. The love of fatherhood and motherhood is a divine revelation and miracle. It is a creative act of God in us. Last year it was not; this year it is, and all things are changed. The dry dock of our selfishness has been struck and the water of sacrificial love pours forth. The thorn bush is aflame with a beautiful fire that does not consume. The springing up of this new force of love is essential for the very existence of human society. Unless it were promptly forthcoming, children would die like the flies of later summer and the race would perish.

These family affections are the most striking and powerful forms of human love. They have the support of physical nearness and of constant intercourse and habit. But the social impulse of the race is just as truly at work in the keen interest we take in a chance-met stranger, in the cheer we feel in meeting a boyhood friend, in the sense of comradeship with those who work or play alongside of us. Every normal man has uncounted relations of good will, and the mobility of modern life has immensely increased the contacts for most of us.

Love takes on as many forms in society as life assumes in vegetation. When it turns toward the strong and noble we call it admiration. When it turns down toward the helpless we call it pity and compassion. The sense of obligation and sympathy that draws young men and women to share the life of the poor or the backward races is love. The loyalty we feel for the great leaders in politics or war, for the masters of science, poetry, or wisdom, is a specialized form of love.

Almost every personal relation of affection connects us with a group of people who have the same interest or who are somehow identified with persons whom we love. So the love for one man promptly widens out into the love of many and weaves more closely the web of social life.

But many of our loves are directly for groups and organizations of men—for our church, our lodge, our fraternity, our college, our party. All such relationships are strong in just the degree in which they evoke love. The cohesion of selfishness is brittle. Selfishness sticks while it feeds, and then wipes its mouth and turns away. Love alone creates enduring loyalties and persuades the individual to give up something of his own for the common good of society. Therefore all organizations cultivate loyalty and the team spirit. "The team spirit" is a modern name for the wider, co-operative love.

Still larger than these selective group relations is the patriotic enthusiasm for city, state, and country. In times of common peril or deliverance we realize the enormous power of this vast collective love, which shakes men with fierce emotion and sends them to wounds, sickness, and death. Here, too, love is the real cement of society. The state has the right and power of coercion, but any state that relies chiefly on force is perishable and doomed. Republics may be slovenly and ill-prepared, but they have great staying powers in war, because they are sustained by the love of the people. No state can afford to disregard the disaffection of a large class or the work of any party that substitutes sullenness and contempt for patriotic pride.

Thus love widens out from the jealous desire of a lover who monopolizes the caresses of his beloved, to the large devotion of the great lovers of mankind and the leaders of humane causes. The firm mouth and strong jaws of Washington's portraits do not symbolize love to us like the tender face of the Madonna brooding over her child, but the steadfast devotion with which he lifted his country and his cause through years of strain and fear was an equally sublimated type of love, the love of a strong man who serves his country.

In all its forms love creates an enjoyment of contact and a desire for more of it, a sense of the worth and the human beauty of those we love, pride in their advancement, joy in their happiness, pain in their suffering, a consciousness of unity, an identity of interests, an instinctive realization of solidarity.

This is the wide sense in which we must use the word "love" if we are to realize the incomparable power and value of love in human life. Our understanding of life depends on our comprehension of the universal power of love. Our capacity to build society depends on our power of calling out love. Our faith in God and Christ is measured by our faith in the value and workableness of love.

LOVE AND SOCIAL PROGRESS

Every step of social progress demands an increase in love. The history of evolution is a history of the appearance and the expansion of love. The first dawn of social cohesion appears in the love of parent animals for their young. The sympathetic type emerges as we ascend the scale of life. The offspring of love survive, propagate, and bequeath their capacity for love. Nature, by the power of life and death, weeds out the loveless and increases the totality of love in the universe.

In the history of man social organization began in groups that had common blood and the sense of kinship to bind them. Every enduring enlargement of political organization demands a basis of fellow-feeling, and love as well as common economic interests. Kings and statesmen have tried to patch nations and races together by treaties or coercion, but unless intermarriage has fused the blood, and religion and common suffering have welded the spirits of the people, empires have dropped apart again along the ancient lines of cleavage. The history of the Germans, the Italians, and the Slavs in the nineteenth century and today consists largely of the effort to undo the artificial cobbling and stitching of kingcraft and to allow the nations to coalesce in commonwealths along the lines marked out by national love and race coherence.

We can watch the society-making force of love at work in the creation of new social organizations. Not even a little local trade union nor lodge nor church nor club can be made successful unless there are in its membership some individuals with the higher qualities of enthusiasm and affection. Selfish interests are necessary, too, for durability, but love is the real chemical for amalgamation.

Where new organizations have to overcome resistance and hostility, as in the case of new religious movements or in the labor movement and socialism, the common suffering and the need of sympathetic support of mind by mind create a wonderful fund of fraternal love. Perhaps from the larger point of view of God the selfish opposition of those who resist the movements of the people may be justified by the fact that the labor and the suffering which they impose upon the lower classes evoke love and create solidarity—much as the travail and toil of childbearing bind the mother to her child—and so fits the new social group for future control.

Co-operative organizations are a remarkable demonstration of the society-making power of love. Judged from a financial point of view they have no chance of survival. Those who organize them usually have little capital, little experience, little business ability. The co-operatives are matched against the best survivors of capitalistic competition, and their entrance into the field often causes a united effort of all their competitors to keep them down, while they themselves are forbidden by their principles to undersell the others. Yet with proper management they have slowly built up an international success that commands the increasing admiration of social students. Their strength is in love. They succeed best among the lower classes, who always have to practice interdependence. They utilize strong neighborly feeling, the good will of old acquaintanceship and kinship, or the new loyalty of socialist convictions, and the hatred for exploitation. They do not succeed among classes where every man is for himself, intent on advancing personally and quite willing to leave others behind. The next fifty years will see a long contest for survival and dominion between the capitalistic and the co-operative type of organization. The former is strong through selfishness and possession; the latter through the resources of love.

Thus love is the society-making force. Social progress depends on the available supply of love. If the sense of solidarity is so strong that injustice and oppression are intolerable to all and the creation of new fraternal relations is swift and easy, then society can efficiently meet every new strain. If one large class has no fellow-feeling and conscious regard for another large class, a flaw runs through the girder and it may split under pressure.

THE BREAKDOWN OF LOVE

This is exactly the situation which confronts us in the industrial world in all nations, including our own. Love has failed between great social classes of men. The working class have become doubtful of the identity of interest between them and the employing and possessing class. They feel they are being victimized and not led. They lag in their work. The spontaneous capacities of labor evoked by love lie dormant in them. They feel that they are hirelings and not friends of those who control their lives. They believe the share of the collective wealth which is paid over to them is determined by their own weakness and the legal and economic power of the opposing group, and not by the productive value of their work nor by their human needs.

This interpretation of their relations may be mistaken in detail. Where love is lacking, the atmosphere becomes clouded with suspicion and misunderstandings, and it becomes increasingly hard to see the truth, even for those who desire to see it. But where the area of hostility is so wide, the feeling so bitter, and the fundamental charge of injustice so frequently and clearly substantiated, no excuse or countercharge can settle the question any longer. Jesus says if we become conscious that our brother has a grievance against us, it becomes the prime concern of our mind to make the matter right. Even if the consciousness comes to us when we are engaged in the most solemn and reverential act of religion, we are to drop everything and first heal the broken fellowship and establish love. The upper classes throughout the world are in that position. Their right of occupation and the justice of their stewardship are under challenge. The gravest issue is not simply a question of dollars and cents, but of the sterilization of love by social injustice. If love is really as important to God and humanity as we have said, this social antagonism becomes a very serious thing to a religious mind. Must we permanently live in a loveless industrial world, or do we dare to be Christians?

The frequency with which our communities have to fall back on physical coercion is a symptom of the failure of love, for love can usually dispense with force. The more love, the less force; the more force, the less love. Despotic government had to use plentiful force to keep its unnatural structure erect. The spread of democracy has brought a great softening of the horrors of criminal law and it will yet bring us a great lessening of militarism. Every proposed increase in police force and military organization is a challenge and accusation against those institutions of society which ought to create social solidarity. If ever our country draws toward its ruin, it will bristle with efficient arsenals and hired fighters. The constant use of military violence in labor disputes in our country proves that industry is still in the despotic stage. It needs democratizing and christianizing.

Love and Modern Business

The severest test and the most urgent task of love today is in the field of business life. Unless love can dominate the making of wealth, the wealth of our nation will be the ferment of its decay. There will be no genuine advance for human society until business experiences the impulse, the joy, and the mental fertility of free teamwork. As long as industry is built on fundamental antagonisms and the axle of every wheel is hot with smothered resentment, there can be no reign of love and no new era of civilization. Our age is asking the leaders of the business world to take a great constructive forward step and to found business on organized love. It summons them to be Christians in business. It seems like a leap in the dark. Will they dare?

Every great engineering work is financed by the stored labor of the past. In the same way all moral progress must draw on the reservoir of righteous purpose and human sympathy stored by religion. Is there enough love in our nation to back up a great moral advance?

Whoever utilizes a woman to satisfy his desires, without respecting her soul and her equal human worth, prostitutes her. Whoever utilizes a man to satisfy his desire for wealth, without respecting his soul and his equal human worth, and without realizing the beating heart and hopes of his fellow, prostitutes him. Whoever gives the consent of his mind to getting unearned gain, to getting more from his fellows than he returns to them in service, steps outside of the realm of love. If the law protects semipredatory undertakings it involves all the citizens of a democracy in wrongdoing. If the Church looks on injustice without holy anger it allows the institution of redemptive love to give shelter to lovelessness, and is itself involved in the charge of hypocrisy.

Paul laid on religion the indispensableness of love. The Christian Church must lay the same law on modern business. Thus:

If I create wealth beyond the dream of past ages and increase not love, my heat is the flush of fever and my success will deal death.

Though I have foresight to locate the fountains of riches, and power to pre-empt them, and skill to tap them, and have no loving vision for humanity, I am blind.

Though I give of my profits to the poor and make princely endowments for those who toil for me, if I have no human fellowship of love with them my life is barren and doomed.

Love is just and kind. Love is not greedy and covetous. Love exploits no one; it takes no unearned gain; it gives more than it gets. Love does not break down the lives of others to make wealth for itself; it makes wealth to build the life of all. Love seeks solidarity; it tolerates no divisions; it prefers equal workmates; it shares its efficiency. Love enriches all men, educates all men, gladdens all men.

The values created by love never fail; but whether there are class privileges, they shall fail; whether there are millions gathered, they shall be scattered; and whether there are vested rights, they shall be abolished. For in the past strong men lorded it in ruthlessness and strove for their own power and pride, but when the perfect social order comes, the strong shall serve the common good. Before the sun of Christ brought in the dawn, men competed, and forced tribute from weakness, but when the full day shall come, they will work as mates in love, each for all and all for each. For now we see in the selfishness, darkly, but then with social vision; now we see our fragmentary ends, but then we shall see the destinies of the race as God sees them. But now abideth honor, justice, and love, these three; and the greatest of these is love.

LOVE VALIDATES ITSELF

Love carries its own validation. It proves its own efficiency and trustworthiness in action. Selfishness always looks safe; love always looks like an enormous risk. But many a man has found that when all his other securities had depreciated, love still paid dividends. Those who are too timid to embark in some venture of love are finally left on the desert shores of a life without interest or hope.

We never live so intensely as when we love strongly. We never realize ourselves so vividly as when we are in the full glow of love for others.

Love establishes the fullest intellectual contact with the world about us. It has a passionate desire for full comprehension, whereas selfishness loses interest as soon as it has made the other serve its ends. To understand things and people we must love them. Love is the greatest educator, the most permanent stimulus of the intellectual life. The animals that stand out among others by their intelligence—the dog, the ant, the bee, the elephant—are all social and gregarious beings; a beast that lives a solitary life must have incessant training to learn a few poor tricks. A selfish person becomes a stupid person if he lives long enough. Other things being equal, the loving people are the wise people. Selfishness grinds a thin edge on the mind but this edge turns and then makes a ragged cut. Love has the keenest insight and yet does not hurt. Selfish cleverness sees keenly the surface mechanisms of life which it wants to manipulate; love instinctively imparts the deeper secrets and imparts the deeper secrets and larger meanings of God's world. The light of true wisdom does not fall on the facts of life from any outward source; it is shed only from the inner eye of him who beholds them, and if his inner eye is darkened, there is no wisdom in all the world for him.

Love demands sacrifice, and sacrifice seems the denial and surrender of life. Actually love is the great intensifier of life and giving our life preserves it. By seeking life selfishly, we lose it; when we lose it for love we gain it. We are far more active and self-assertive when we impart than when we receive. It is literally true that "it is more blessed to give than to receive."

When people have lived for forty years and their desires begin to flag, the great test of age arrives. If they have launched young bodies and minds on the great adventurous cruise of life, there are still for them the hoisting of pennants, the slap of the open sea, the foreboding of the storm, the pride of the successful homeward run. If they have identified themselves for years with some cause of humanity—the cause of temperance or purity or peace or justice—working for it and suffering for it, their lives will have a meaning and a hope and a great pride to the end. But if they have fed no life but their own, have no investments except dollars and must pay for all the sympathy they get, they are locked in a gray prison which they have built for themselves. Such lives are truly old, even if their bodies are kept young by all the skill that money buys. They have lost the fundamental contacts with the world. If we knew the profound loneliness and monotony of many people who have preferred wealth to the burdens and risks of love, we should not dash for the bait which they gorged.

On the other hand love rejuvenates life. When, occasionally, old people take a new plunge into love, they grow so young and dapper that everybody laughs. We can watch the same wonder when a child comes to people who have longed for one for years. So love is the fountain of youth which the Spanish conquistadores sought. It was located in America after all, but, being "conquerors," they could never have found it.

Jesus said that love is the supreme law of life and the thing men live by. Love validates the assertion. It pays as it goes. Nothing else does pay in the long run. The more true happiness and abiding satisfaction we have had from love, the more ought we to trust it as the true way of life.

THE OUTCOME

If, now, love is so all-pervasive and manifold in the life of humanity; if it is indeed the indispensable condition for the existence and progress of society; if it has proved its constructive value and superior efficiency whenever it has received a fair test, then I ask all who have followed these thoughts to the end to affirm with me their faith in love and to make a new committal to the cause of establishing love on earth. We must not only accept it and enjoy it when it comes to us, but we must seek it, cultivate it, and propagate it like health, wealth, and education. It is not an incidental blessing, but the first and fundamental law of God, written in our hearts, and written large in all the world about us. When we heal love that has been torn, remove all contradictions of love from the outward relations of our life and allow love to become our second nature, we shall deserve the highest patent of nobility—to be called sons of God. If love involves loss, we must accept the loss. Christ did. If selfishness seems to work better than love, we must have faith in love. Just as a businessman invests money for years in a business proposition because he has faith in it, so we must stake our fortune on love and feel sure of coming out ahead in the venture. Why else do the significance of Christianity.

LOVE AND CHRISTIANITY

From this sunlit hilltop of reflection we may gain a fresh vision of the significance of Christianity.

A man is a Christian in the degree in which he shares the spirit and consciousness of Jesus Christ, conceiving God as Jesus knew him and seeing human life as Jesus realized it. None of us has ever done this fully, but on the other hand there is no man within the domain of Christendom who has not been influenced by Christ in some way.

Now Jesus with incomparable spiritual energy set love into the center of religion. He drove home the duty of love with words so mighty that our race can never again forget them. He embodied the principle of love in the undying charm and youthful strength of his own life in such a way as to exert an assimilating compulsion over more lives than we can number. He was conscious of God as a sunny and lovable presence and he taught his friends to think of God as a father who loved them unselfishly and wanted nothing from them except love. This conception of God was reinforced when men saw in the cross the great declaration of the redemptive love of God.

As the outcome of the life and death of Jesus, a body of organized life and thought was set in motion through history which interpreted the universe from the point of view of love and saw all ethical questions and duties with love at the center. If this movement had died out in the second century but its literature had been preserved, all thoughtful men today, of every school of philosophy, would point to it as the fairest and most brilliant venture ever made in the field of morals and religion. But it did not die. It has such religious vitality and organizing force that it survived and spread. Though only a fragment of its original faith was dissolved and embodied in the institutions of society, it made the nations that adopted it the dominant nations of the earth. Every time that faith was cleansed of its foreign contaminations, every time more of its force was released and embodied in social life, the history of Western civilization dated a new epoch. In spite of all failures the Christian religion has been the one organized force in the Western world which has consciously sought to increase love.

Christianity stands for the belief that "God is love." It has succeeded in making that tremendous assertion of faith a commonplace. In so far as we have taken that doctrine seriously it has revolutionized our spiritual outlook and put a new face on the universe.

Christianity stands for the doctrine that we must love one another—all men, without distinction of "religion, race, color or previous condition of servitude." It will tolerate no exempt breed of supermen and no pre-empted areas of God's common world. It does not call on the strong to climb to isolation across the backs of the weak, but challenges them to prove their strength by lifting the rest with them. It does not advise eliminating the unfit, but seeks to make them fit. It stands for the solidarity of the race in its weakness and strength, its defeats and conquests, its sin and salvation.

If love is the greatest thing in the world and if it is the prime condition of social progress, what of the Christian religion, which has identified itself with faith in love?

Every man can profit by the historical influences of Christianity and be a passive pensioner on its vested funds. But it clearly needs active personal agents who will incarnate its vitalities, propagate its principles, liberate its undeveloped forces, purify its doctrine, and extend the sway of its faith in love over new realms of social life. Dare we be such men? Dare we be Christians? Those who take up the propaganda of love and substitute freedom and fraternity for coercion and class differences in social life are the pioneers of the Kingdom of God; for the reign of the God of love will be fulfilled in a life of humanity organized on the basis of solidarity and love.

* VI *

The Social Principles of Jesus

*I*N 1915 a group of large American banks made loans to Great Britain and France, enabling them to buy munitions and supplies in the United States. Transcontinental telephone service was established. In 1916 the federal income tax was declared constitutional by the Supreme Court. The United States invaded Mexico. A good-roads bill was passed by Congress.

These were Billy Sunday's big years. The popular evangelist drew large crowds in cities, in specially-built tabernacles. Billy had said "Goodbye to Baseball," adding, "I'm going to Jesus Christ." Billy exhorted converts to stay away from card games and beer. (There were long parades against the saloon.) Part of the press called him "coarse and vulgar," but he was defended because of his ability as an orator by Lyman Abbott in the Outlook.

Churches intensified their relief work for victims of war and became involved in the discussion of the merits of the cause of the Allies. The possibility of American involvement in the war was being considered. At the same time more church people showed interest in campaigns against child labor.

In 1916 Association Press, the publishing agency of the International Committee of Young Men's Christian Associations, New York, published as one of a series of "college voluntary study courses" a book by Rauschenbusch under the title The Social Principles of Jesus. It was described by him as "not a life of Christ, nor an exposition of his religious teachings, nor a doctrinal statement about his person and work. It is an attempt to formulate in simple propositions the fundamental convictions of Jesus about the social and ethical relations and duties of men." He would sum up "the principles which we must understand if we are to follow Jesus in the way of life. . . ." The work was written under the direction of a subcommittee on college courses of the Sunday School council of evangelical denominations and the committee

89

on voluntary study of the Council of North American Student Movements.

As early as 1895 Rauschenbusch had published in German The Life of Jesus. This later study course prepared in his most mature years, several years before his death, illustrates his method of continuous study of the Bible. He was as "biblical" as any man who ever wrote on religious subjects in his day or other days, and surely as biblical as later dissenters from his theses.

By 1916 it was evident that the modern world was in the midst not only of a tremendous armed conflict but also of widespread social upheaval. In the midst of the great controversies that raged in the United States prior to the entry of the United States into the conflict, Rauschenbusch went into a thorough reinterpretation of his great theme, the teachings of Jesus in relation to social forces and conditions. In his references to current controversies he was always reminding the reader of the evils that are caused by unjust social conditions.

In this book Rauschenbusch wrote twelve chapters under four sections entitled "The Axiomatic Social Convictions of Jesus," "The Social Ideal of Jesus," "The Recalcitrant Social Forces," "Conquest by Conflict." In the last he dealt with the conflict with evil and the cross of Christ as a social principle. The final chapter, a review and a challenge, with the subtitle "The Social Principles of Jesus Demand Personal Allegiance and Social Action," appears here almost in full text.

✳

The Social Mission of Christians

"Ye are the salt of the earth. . . . Ye are the light of the world." [Matt. 5:13, 14.]

Jesus speaks here with the consciousness of an historic mission to the whole of humanity. Yet it was a Nazarene carpenter speaking to a group of Galilean peasants and fishermen. Under the circumstances, and at the time, it was an utterance of the most daring faith—faith in himself, faith in them, faith in what he was putting into them, faith in faith. Jesus failed and was crucified, first his body by his enemies, and then his spirit by the men who bore his name. But that failure was so amazing a success that today it takes an effort on our part to realize that it required any faith on his part to inaugurate the Kingdom of God and to send out his apostolate.[1]

If the antiseptic and enlightening influence of the sincere followers

[1] Christianity and the Social Crisis, 415.

of Jesus were eliminated from our American communities, what would be the presumable social effects?

The Great Initiator of the Kingdom of God

At that season Jesus answered and said, I thank thee, O Father, Lord of heaven and earth, that thou didst hide these things from the wise and understanding, and didst reveal them unto babes: yea, Father, for so it was well-pleasing in thy sight. All things have been delivered unto me of my Father: and no one knoweth the Son, save the Father; neither doth any know the Father, save the Son, and he to whomsoever the Son willeth to reveal him. Come unto me, all ye that labor and are heavy laden, and I will give you rest. Take my yoke upon you, and learn of me; for I am meek and lowly in heart: and ye shall find rest unto your souls. For my yoke is easy, and my burden is light. [Matt. 11:25–30.]

This is one of the most thrilling passages in the Bible. It has always been understood as a call to intimate religion, as the appeal of a personal Saviour to those who are loaded with sin and weary of worldliness. But in fact it expresses the sense of a revolutionary mission to society.

Jesus had the consciousness of a unique relation to the Father, which made him the mediator of a new understanding of God and of life (v. 27). This new insight was making a new intellectual alignment, leaving the philosophers and scholars as they were, and fertilizing the minds of simple people (v. 25). It is an historical fact that the brilliant body of intellectuals of the first and second centuries was blind to what proved to be the most fruitful and influential movement of all times, and it was left to slaves and working men to transmit it and save it from suppression at the cost of their lives.

Then Jesus turns to the toiling and heavy-laden people about him with the offer of a new kind of leadership—none of the brutal self-assertion of the Caesars and of all conquerors here, but a gentle and humble spirit, and an obedience which was pleasure and brought release to the soul.

These words express his consciousness of being different, and of bearing within him the beginnings of a new spiritual constitution of humanity.

When individuals have really come under the new law of Christ, does Jesus make good?

Would he also make good if humanity based its collective life on the social principles which we have studied?

If the choice is between Caesar and Christ, which shall it be?

The Kingdom of Truth

Pilate therefore entered again into the Praetorium, and called Jesus, and said unto him, Art thou the King of the Jews? Jesus answered, Sayest thou this of thyself, or did others tell it thee concerning me? Pilate answered, Am I a Jew? Thine own nation and the chief priests delivered thee unto me: what hast thou done? Jesus answered, My kingdom is not of this world: if my kingdom were of this world, then would my servants fight, that I should not be delivered to the Jews: but now is my kingdom not from hence. Pilate therefore said unto him, Art thou a king then? Thou sayest that I am a king. To this end have I been born, and to this end am I come into the world, that I should bear witness unto the truth. Every one that is of the truth heareth my voice. Pilate saith unto him, What is truth? And when he had said this, he went out again unto the Jews, and saith unto them, I find no crime in him. [John 18:33–38.]

All kingdoms rest on force; formerly on swords and bayonets, now on big guns. To overthrow them you must prepare more force, bigger guns. Jesus was accused before Pilate of being leader of a force revolution aiming to make him king. He claimed the kingship, but repudiated the force. To his mind the absence of force resistance was characteristic of his whole undertaking. Instead, his power was based on the appeal and attractiveness of truth. When Pilate heard about "truth" he thought he had a sophist before him, one more builder of metaphysical systems, and expressed the skepticism of the man on the street: "What is truth?" But Jesus was not a teacher of abstract doctrine, whatever his expounders have made of him. His mind was bent on realities. If we substitute "reality" for "truth" in his saying here, we shall get near his thought.

Which is more durable, power based on force, or power based on spiritual coherence?

A Mental Transformation

I beseech you therefore, brethren, by the mercies of God, to present your bodies a living sacrifice, holy, acceptable to God, which is your spiritual service. And be not fashioned according to this world: but be ye transformed by the renewing of your mind, that ye may prove what is the good and acceptable and perfect will of God. [Rom. 12:1, 2.]

In the first century the Christians were a new social group, confronting the social order of the Roman Empire with a new religious faith, a revolutionary hope, and a powerful impulse of fraternity. Those who had come out of pagan society still felt the pull of its loose pleasures and moral maxims, and of its idolatry. Paul here challenges them to submit fully to the social assimilation of the new group. It involved an intellectual renewal, a new spiritual orientation, which must have been searching and painful. It involved the loss of many social pleasures, of business profit and civic honor, and it might at any time mean banishment, torture, and death. The altar symbol of sacrifice might become a scarlet reality. Yet see with what triumphant joy and assurance Paul speaks.

If a student should dedicate himself to the creation of a Christian social order today, would it still require an intellectual renewing?

Would it cramp him or enlarge him?

The Distinctive Contribution of Christ

There was the true light, even the light which lighteth every man, coming into the world. He was in the world, and the world was made through him, and the world knew him not. He came unto his own, and they that were his own received him not. But as many received him, to them gave he the right to become children of God, even to them that believe on his name: who were born, not of blood, nor of the will of the flesh, nor of the will of man, but of God. And the Word became flesh, and dwelt among us (and we beheld his glory, glory as of the only begotten from the Father), full of grace and truth. For the law was given through Moses; grace and truth came through Jesus Christ. [John 1:9–14, 17.]

Here is the tragedy of the Gospel story, seen from a long perspective and stated in terms of Greek philosophy. The Light which lighteth every man, the Logos through whom God had created the kosmos, had come to this world in human form, and been rejected. But some had received him, and these had received a new life through him, which made them children of God. They had discovered in him a new kind of spiritual splendor, characterized by "grace and truth." Even Moses had contributed only law to humanity; Christ was identified with grace and truth.

How would you paraphrase the statements of John to express the attitude of nineteen centuries to Christ?

What has he in fact done for those who have received him?

What would be the modern equivalent of "grace and truth" to express the distinctive contribution of Christ to human history?

The Master of the Greatest Game

Therefore let us also, seeing we are compassed about with so great a cloud of witnesses, lay aside every weight, and the sin which doth so easily beset us, and let us run with patience the race that is set before us, looking unto Jesus the author and perfecter of our faith, who for the joy that was set before him endured the cross, despising shame, and hath sat down at the right hand of the throne of God. For consider him that hath endured such gainsaying of sinners against himself, that ye wax not weary, fainting in your souls. [Heb. 12:1–3.]

The man who wrote the little treatise from which this is quoted saw the history of humanity summed up in the live spirits who had the power of projection into the future. Faith is the quality of mind which sees things before they are visible, which acts on ideals before they are realities, and which feels the distant city of God to be more dear, substantial, and attractive than the edible and profitable present. Read Hebrews 11. So he calls on Christians to take up the same manner of life, and compares them with men running a race in an amphitheater packed with all the generations of the past who are watching them make their record. But he bids them keep their eye on Jesus who starts them at the line and will meet them at the goal, and who has set the pace for good and fleet men for all time.

What is the social and evolutionary value of the men of "faith" in the sense of Hebrews 11?

Have we left Jesus behind us by this time?

The Beginning of the Greatest Movement in History

Now after John was delivered up, Jesus came into Galilee, preaching the gospel of God, and saying, The time is fulfilled, and the kingdom of God is at hand: repent ye, and believe in the gospel.

And passing along by the sea of Galilee, he saw Simon and Andrew the brother of Simon casting a net in the sea; for they were fishers. And Jesus said unto them, Come ye after me, and I will make you to become fishers of men. And straightway they left the nets, and followed him. And going on a little further, he saw James the son of Zebedee, and John his brother, who also were in the boat mending the nets. And straightway he called them: and they left their father Zebedee in the boat with the hired servants, and went after him. [Mark 1:14–20.]

Here we have the beginning of organized Christianity. This is the germinal cell of that vast social movement of which foreign missions, the establishment of the American Republic, and the modern labor movement are products. It began with repentance, faith, and self-sacrificing action, and it will always have to advance by the same means. To those four men Jesus was an incarnate challenge. He dared them to come, and promised to put their lives on a higher level. He stands over against us with the same challenge. He points to the blackened fields of battle, to the economic injustice and exploitation of industry, to the paganism and sexualism of our life. Is this old order of things to go on forever? Will our children, and their children, still be ground through the hopper? Or have we faith to adventure our life in a new order, the Kingdom of God?

Has our study of the "Social Principles of Jesus" revealed a clear and consistent scheme of life, worthy of our respect?

Three convictions were axiomatic with Jesus, so that all his reasoning and his moral imperatives were based on them, just as all thought and work in physics is based on gravitation. These convictions were the sacredness of life and personality, the solidarity of the human family, and the obligation of the strong to stand up for all whose life is impaired or whose place within humanity is denied.

It cannot be questioned that these convictions were a tremendous and spontaneous force in the spirit of Jesus. That alone suffices to align him with all idealistic minds, to whom man is more than matter, more than labor force, a mysterious participant of the spiritual powers of the universe. It aligns him with all men of solidaristic conviction, who are working for genuine community life in village and city, for a nation with fraternal institutions and fraternal national consciousness, and for a coming family of nations and races. It aligns him with all exponents of the democratic social spirit of our day, who feel the wrongs of the common people and are trying to make the world juster and more fraternal.

The best forces of modern life are converging along these lines. There is no contradiction between them and the spirit of Jesus. On the contrary, they are largely the product of his spirit, diffused and organized in the Western world. He was the initiator; we are the interpreters and agents. Nor has he been outstripped like an early inventor and discoverer whose crude work is honored only because others were able to improve on it. Quite the contrary; the more vividly these spiritual convictions glow in the heart of any man, the more will he feel that Jesus is still ahead, still the inspiring force. As soon as we get beyond theory to life and action, we know that we are dependent for the spiritual powers in modern life on the continued influence of Jesus Christ over the lives of others.

In the second place, Jesus had a social ideal, the Reign of God on earth, in which God's will would be done. This ideal with him was not a Utopian and academic fancy, but the great prize and task of life toward which he launched all his energies. He called men to turn away from the evil ways of the old order, and to get a mind fit for the new. He set the able individuals to work, and put the spirit of intense labor and devotion into them. He proposed to effect the transition from the old order to the new by expanding the area of moral obligation and raising the standards of moral relationships.

By having such a social ideal at all, he draws away from all who are stationary and anchored in the world as it is; from all who locate the possibility of growth and progress in the individual only; and from all whose desire for perfection runs away from this world to a world beyond the grave.

By moving toward the new social order of the Kingdom of God with such wholeness of determination, he is the constant rebuke for all of us who are trying to live with a "divided allegiance," straddling between the iniquities of force, profit, and inhumanity, and the fraternal righteousness of the Gospel we profess to believe. Jesus at least was no time-server, no Mr. Facing-both-ways, no hypocrite; and whenever we touch his elbow by inadvertence, a shiver of reality and self-contempt runs through us.

In the third place, Jesus dealt with serious intelligence with the great human instincts that go wrong.

The capacity for leadership and the desire for it have fastened the damning institutions of tyranny and oppression on humanity and tied us up so completely that the rare historical chances of freedom and progress have been like a tumultuous and brief escape. Yet Jesus saw that ambition was not to be suppressed, but to be yoked to the service of society. In the past, society was allowed to advance and prosper only if this advanced the prosperity and security of its ruling classes. Jesus proposed that this be reversed, so that the leaders would have to earn power and honor by advancing the welfare of society by distinguished service at cost to themselves.

The desire for private property has been the chief outlet for selfish impulses antagonistic to public welfare. To gain private wealth men have slaughtered the forests, contaminated the rivers, drained the fertility of the soil, monopolized the mineral wealth of the country, enslaved childhood, double-yoked motherhood, exhausted manhood, hog-tied community undertakings, and generally acted as the dog in the manger toward humanity. Jesus opposed accumulation without moral purpose, the inhumanity of property differences, and the fatal absorption of money-making. Yet he was not ascetic. It is probably safe to say that he would not be against private property in so far as it serves the common good, and not against public property at all.

Like ambition and the property instinct, the religious impulse may go wrong, and subject society to its distortions or tyranny. Jesus always stood for an ethical and social outcome of religion. He sought to harness the great power of religion to righteousness and love. With a mind so purely religious we might expect that he would make all earthly and social interests subservient to personal religion. The fact that he reversed it, seems clear proof that he was socially minded and that the Kingdom of God as a right social organism was the really vital thing to him.

Finally, Jesus had a deep sense of the sin and evil in the world. Human nature is frail; men of evil will are powerful; organized evil is in practical control. Consequently social regeneration involves not only growth but conflict. The way to the Kingdom of God always has been and always will be a *via dolorosa*. The cross is not accidental, but is a law of social progress.

These conceptions together seem to shape up into a consistent conception of social life. It is not the modern scientific scheme, but a religious view of life. But it blends incomparably better with modern science than the scholastic philosophy or theology of an age far nearer to us than Jesus. It is strange how little modern knowledge has to discount in the teachings of Jesus. As Romanes once pointed out,[2] Plato followed Socrates and lived amidst a blaze of genius never since equaled; he is the greatest representative of human reason in the direction of spirituality unaided by revelation; "but the errors in the dialogues reach to absurdity in reason and to sayings shocking to the moral sense."

The writer of this little book has come back to an intensive study of Jesus at intervals of years, and every time it was like a fresh revelation, leaving a sense of mental exhilaration and a new sense of joy in truth. Never was there a feeling that Jesus was exhausted and had nothing more to say.

For a true valuation of his intellectual contribution to mankind we must remember that we have not a page of his own writing. We are dependent on the verbal memory of his own disciples; so far as we know, nothing was written down for years. The fragments which survived probably had to stand the ordeal of translation from the Aramaic to the Greek. Simply from the point of view of literature, it is an amazing thing that anything characteristic in Jesus survived at all. But it did. His sayings have the sparkle of genius and personality; the illustrations and epigrams which he threw off in fertile profusion are still clinchers; even his humor plays around them. Critics undertake to fix on the genuine sayings by internal evidence. Only a mind of transcendent orginality could win its way to posterity through such obstructions.

But we ought not to forget the brevity of our material when we try

[2] G. J. Romanes, *Thoughts on Religion*, 157.

to build up a coherent conception of his outlook on society. There is little use in stickling on details. The main thing is the personality of Jesus, his religious and ethical insight into the nature and needs of the social life of mankind, the vital power of religious conviction which he was able to put behind righteousness, and the historical force which he set going through history.

From the indirect influences which Jesus Christ set in motion, no man or woman or child in America can escape. We live on him. Even those who attack the Christian Church, or who repudiate what they suppose Christ to stand for, do so with spiritual weapons which they have borrowed from him. But it does make a great difference whether the young men and women of our day give their conscious and intelligent allegiance to Christianity or hold aloof in misunderstanding. Without them the Christian movement will mark time on old issues. With them it will dig new irrigation channels and string the wires for new power transmission.

In return, Christianity can do more for students than they themselves are likely to realize in youth. Men grow tired. Their moral enthusiasm flags. Scientific sociology may remain academic, cold, and ineffective. We need inspiration, impulse, will power, and nothing can furnish such steady accessions of moral energy as living religion. Science and the Christian faith combined are strong. Those who succeed in effecting a combination of these two without insincerity or cowardice are the coming leaders.

If a student's mind has given inward consent to the teachings of Jesus in this course of study, that constitutes an appeal for personal discipleship. Can we go with Christ in living out these principles, and meanwhile draw on his spiritual wealth to build up our growing life? If there is a student who cannot at present affirm all that the Christian Church holds concerning the nature of Christ, why should he not approach him as the earliest disciples did, by personal love and obedience, following him and co-operating with him in the business of the Kingdom of God, and arriving in time at full faith in his Messiahship? A great and firm faith is the product and prize of a lifetime of prayer and loving action. "Light is sown to the righteous." As we gather the wisdom of life, and find that while we move from knowledge to knowledge, we are also advancing from mystery to mystery, many of us will be ready and glad to join in the highest affirmation of faith about Jesus Christ, in whom we have learned to see God.

> If Jesus Christ is a man,
> And only a man, I say

That of all mankind I cleave to him,
And to him I cleave alway.

If Jesus Christ is a God,
And the only God, I swear
I will follow him through heaven and hell,
The earth, the sea, and the air.
                    —*Richard Watson Gilder*

If Christianity henceforth is to discharge its full energy in the regeneration of social life, it especially needs the allegiance of college men and women who have learned to understand to some degree the facts and laws of human society. The development of what is called "Social Christianity" or "the social gospel" is a fusion between the new understanding created by the social sciences, and the teachings and moral ideals of Christianity. This combination was inevitable; it has already registered social effects of the highest importance; if it can win the active minds of the present generation of college students, it will swing a part of the enormous organized forces of the Christian Church to bear on the social tasks of our American communities, and that will help to create the nobler America which we see by faith.

Christians have never fully understood Christianity. A purer comprehension of its tremendous contents is always necessary. Think what it would signify to a local community if all sincere Christian people in it should interpret their obligation in the social terms which we have been using; if they should seek not only their own salvation, but the reign of God in their own town; if they should cultivate the habit of seeing a divine sacredness in every personality, should assist in creating the economic foundations for fraternal solidarity, and if, as Christians, they should champion the weak in their own community. We need a power of renewal in our American communities that will carry us across the coming social transition, and social Christianity can supply it by directing the plastic force of the old faith of our fathers to the new social tasks.

Jesus was the initiator of the Kingdom of God. It is a real thing, now in operation. It is within us, and among us, gaining ground in our intellectual life and in our social institutions. It overlaps and interpenetrates all existing organizations, raising them to a higher level when they are good, resisting them when they are evil, quietly revolutionizing the old social order and changing it into the new. It suffers terrible reverses; we are in the midst of one now; but after a time it may become apparent that a master hand has turned the situation and laid the basis of victory on the wrecks of defeat. The Kingdom of God is always coming; you can never lay your hand on it and say, "It is here." But such fragmentary realizations of it as we have, alone make life worth living. The memories which are still sweet and dear when the fire begins to die in the ashes, are the memories of days when we lived fully in the Kingdom of Heaven, toiling for it, suffering for it, and feeling the stirring of the Godlike and eternal life within us. The most humiliating and crushing realization is that we have betrayed our heavenly Fatherland and sold out for thirty pieces of silver. We often mistake it. We think we see its banner in the distance, when it is only the bloody flag of the old order. But a man learns. He comes to know whether he is in God's country, especially if he sees the great Leader near him.

SUGGESTIONS FOR THOUGHT AND DISCUSSION

I. *The Social Principles of Jesus*

1. Sum up the social principles of Jesus which we have worked out.
2. Do they seem incisive? Would they demand far-reaching social changes? What changes?
3. What conceptions acquired in philosophical and social science studies connect fruitfully with the principles of Jesus? Do any scientific conceptions conflict with the essential ideas of Jesus?

II. *Social Salvation*

1. What is your frank estimate of the value of the social principles of Jesus as a religious and ethical basis for the regeneration of society?
2. Does the spiritual development of modern life tend toward the position of Jesus or away from it?
3. What opportunities and methods does modern life offer for carrying out these principles in our social order?
4. If society cannot be saved under the spiritual leadership of Jesus, how can it be saved?

III. *The Leader*

1. As this course proceeded, has our respect or reverence for Jesus Christ increased or diminished? In what ways?
2. Would it be possible to join the forward Christian forces in working for the Kingdom of God even if the theological questions are still unsolved in our minds?
3. What seem now the best methods of carrying out these principles in our own community and in the world?

IV. *For Special Discussion*

1. Does the salvation of society seem to make the salvation of the individual unnecessary or trivial? Have you lost interest in it?
2. How should social and personal salvation connect?
3. What would a loyal religious dedication to Christ and Christianity mean to our scientific social intelligence?
4. What would it mean to the course of our life?

* VII *

A Theology for the Social Gospel

*I*N 1917 the United States entered the war. Prices, which had risen under the stimulus of the purchases in America by the Allies, rose further. Herbert Hoover was appointed food commissioner and the price of wheat was set. Voluntary rationing of coal, sugar, and other products went into effect. The offices of the Industrial Workers of the World were raided. President Wilson placed the railroads under federal control. The tide for prohibition advanced rapidly. In September, 1917, came war-time prohibition, not to be confused with that brought later by the adoption of the 18th Amendment.

Most of the churches readily supported President Wilson's statement of war aims, and caught up his slogan, "make the world safe for democracy." Soon the churches were actively involved in supporting the war work of the Red Cross and the Christian Associations. The need of feeding child victims of the war made an especial appeal and a Commission on the War and the Religious Outlook began to make studies. Conscientious objectors were summarily imprisoned and received slight sympathy from organized religion except from the historic peace churches, Friends, Brethren, Mennonites.

The American public became intensely anti-German. Fritz Kreisler, the violinist, was not permitted to play classical music. Sauerkraut was named "liberty cabbage." There was sharp criticism of certain churches that still conducted divine worship in the German language. This popular psychology affected local church activity, which became more overtly patriotic.

Rauschenbusch's writing in 1917 was in the same tenor as that of the 1880's and 1907. The churches, he contended, were cultivating personal piety, while discounting the need of social reconstruction, for which he made his pleas. He had received much encouragement from the more numerous social pronouncements of church bodies, the speeches and writings of fellow prophets. But he remained the critical prophet bidding for support. He was getting it effectively from only a minority. In 1917 he went headlong into use of the term "social gospel," which he, of course, did not invent or discover. In his earlier writings he had used largely other terms. Now, in a series of lectures at a theological seminary, he used the term freely.

In the late 1890's Rauschenbusch had written that "we need a theological basis for our social interest." At New Haven in 1917 he gave four lectures, subsequently elaborated for publication in the book, A Theology for the Social Gospel (New York, The Macmillan Company, 1917).

The traditional theology had been, as before observed, both deductive and individualistic. Rauschenbusch's plea was that a great thought had been obscured—"the vast idea of the Kingdom of God . . . and the center of the Gospel."

His lectures were delivered in April, 1917, the month that the Congress declared war on Germany, and little more than a year before he died. He wrote, of course, also in a world in which organized labor had not yet come to power, and the people still held limited concepts of the role of government in the national economy. (See notes before the excerpts from Christianity and the Social Crisis, above.)

To later happenings in church and theological circles, a compiler's note can only refer. There were to be reactions against the social gospel, and its advocates were to become minorities, often small. Certain of Rauschenbusch's followers were criticized for their undue optimism, although obviously Rauschenbusch was no optimist. During the great depression of the 1930's church officials again pronounced boldly in the strain of a Rauschenbusch. But many social liberals in the churches appeared to be perplexed, if not disillusioned, as they contemplated the resistance to social thought among theologians, church officials, ministers, and laity. Nevertheless, Rauschenbusch had undoubtedly influenced many individuals who continued a ferment of discussion in line with that which he had initiated. Indeed, in activistic America most religious bodies have come to recognize some social obligation. Could it have been that the teacher of Rochester has both directly influenced many individuals, and that he and they have indirectly influenced the institutions of religion? At least there are again indications of a swing toward emphases stressed by the lecturer of 1917.

Selections from three chapters follow.

*

FOREWORD

IN APRIL, 1917, I had the honor of delivering four lectures on the Nathaniel W. Taylor Foundation before the Annual Convocation of the Yale School of Religion. These lectures are herewith presented in elaborated form.

The Taylor Lectures are expected to deal with some theme in Doctrinal Theology, but the Faculty in their invitation indicated that a discussion of some phase of the social problem would be welcome. I have tried to obey this suggestion and still to remain well within the original purpose of the Foundation by taking as my subject, "A Theology for the Social Gospel."

Of my qualifications for this subject I have reason to think modestly, for I am not a doctrinal theologian either by professional training or by personal habits of mind. Professional duty and intellectual liking have made me a teacher of church history, and the events of my life, interpreted by my religious experiences, have laid the social problems on my mind. On the other hand, it may be that the necessity of approaching systematic theology from the outside may be of real advantage. Theology has often received its most fruitful impulses when secular life and movements have set it new problems.

Of the subject itself I have no cause to speak modestly. Its consideration is of the highest importance for the future of theology and religion. It bristles with intellectual problems. This book had to be written some time, and as far as I know, nobody has yet written it. I offer my attempt until some other man comes along who can plow deeper and straighter.

*

THE CHALLENGE OF THE SOCIAL GOSPEL TO THEOLOGY

WE HAVE a social gospel. We need a systematic theology large enough to match it and vital enough to back it.

This is the main proposition of this book. The first three chapters are to show that a readjustment and expansion of theology, so that it will furnish an adequate intellectual basis for the social gospel, is necessary, feasible, desirable, and legitimate. The remainder of the book offers

concrete suggestions how some of the most important sections of doctrinal theology may be expanded and readjusted to make room for the
religious convictions summed up in "the social gospel."

Some of my readers, who know the age, the tenacity, and the monu-
mental character of theology well, will smile at the audacity of this
proposal. Others, who know theology still better, will treat this venture very seriously. If theology stops growing or is unable to adjust itself to its modern environment and to meet its present tasks, it will
die. Many now regard it as dead. The social gospel needs a theology
to make it effective; but theology needs the social gospel to vitalize it.
The work attempted in this book is doomed to futility if it has only
the personal ideas of the author behind it. It is worthy of consideration
only if the needs of a new epoch are seeking expression in it, and in
that case its personal defects are of slight importance.

The argument of this book is built on the conviction that the social
gospel is a permanent addition to our spiritual outlook and that its
arrival constitutes a stage in the development of the Christian religion.

We need not waste words to prove that the social gospel is being
preached. It is no longer a prophetic and occasional note. It is a novelty
only in backward social or religious communities. The social gospel has
become orthodox.

It is not only preached. It has set new problems for local church
work, and has turned the pastoral and organizing work of the ministry
into new and constructive directions. It has imparted a wider vision and
a more statesmanlike grasp to the foreign mission enterprise. In home
missions its advent was signalized by the publication, in 1885, of *Our
Country* by Josiah Strong. (*Venerabile nomen!*) That book lifted the
entire home mission problem to a higher level. The religious literature
uttering the social gospel is notable both for its volume and its vitality
and conviction. The emotional fervour of the new convictions has
created prayers and hymns of social aspiration, for which the newer
hymn books are making room. Conservative denominations have for-
mally committed themselves to the fundamental ideas of the social
gospel and their practical application. The plans of great interde-
nominational organizations are inspired by it. It has become a constructive force in American politics.

This new orientation, which is observable in all parts of our religious
life, is not simply a prudent adjustment of church methods to changed
conditions. There is religious compulsion behind it. Those who are in
touch with the student population know what the impulse to social
service means to college men and women. It is the most religious

element in the life of many of them. Among ministerial students there
is an almost impatient demand for a proper social outlet. Some hesitate
to enter the regular ministry at all because they doubt whether it will
offer them sufficient opportunity and freedom to utter and apply their
social convictions. For many ministers who have come under the influence of the social gospel in mature years, it has signified a religious
crisis, and where it has been met successfully, it has brought fresh joy
and power, and a distinct enlargement of mind. It has taken the place
of conventional religion in the lives of many outside the Church. It
constitutes the moral power in the propaganda of socialism.

All those social groups which distinctly face toward the future, clearly
show their need and craving for a social interpretation and application
of Christianity. Whoever wants to hold audiences of working people
must establish some connection between religion and their social feel-
ings and experiences. The religious organizations dealing with college
men and women know that any appeal which leaves out the social
note is likely to meet a listless audience. The most effective evangelists
for these two groups are men who have thoroughly embodied the social gospel in their religious life and thought. When the great evangelistic effort of the "Men and Religion Forward Movement" was
first planned, its organizers made room for "Social Service" very hesi-
tatingly. But as soon as the movement was tried out before the public,
it became clear that only the meetings which offered the people the
social application of religion were striking fire and drawing crowds.

The Great War has dwarfed and submerged all other issues, including our social problems. But in fact the war is the most acute and
tremendous social problem of all. All whose Christianity has not been
ditched by the catastrophe are demanding a christianizing of international relations. The demand for disarmament and permanent peace,
for the rights of the small nations against the imperialistic and colonizing powers, for freedom of the seas and of trade routes, for orderly
settlement of grievances—these are demands for social righteousness
and fraternity on the largest scale. Before the War the social gospel
dealt with social classes; today it is being translated into international
terms. The ultimate cause of the war was the same lust for easy and
unearned gain which has created the internal social evils under which
every nation has suffered. The social problem and the war problem are
fundamentally one problem, and the social gospel faces both. After
the War the social gospel will "come back" with pent-up energy and
clearer knowledge.

The social movement is the most important ethical and spiritual
movement in the modern world, and the social gospel is the response

of the Christian consciousness to it. Therefore it had to be. The social gospel registers the fact that for the first time in history the spirit of Christianity has had a chance to form a working partnership with real social and psychological science. It is the religious reaction on the historic advent of democracy. It seeks to put the democratic spirit, which the Church inherited from Jesus and the prophets, once more in control of the institutions and teachings of the Church.[1]

The social gospel is the old message of salvation, but enlarged and intensified. The individualistic gospel has taught us to see the sinfulness of every human heart and has inspired us with faith in the willingness and power of God to save every soul that comes to him. But it has not given us an adequate understanding of the sinfulness of the social order and its share in the sins of all individuals within it. It has not evoked faith in the will and power of God to redeem the permanent institutions of human society from their inherited guilt of oppression and extortion. Both our sense of sin and our faith in salvation have fallen short of the realities under its teaching. The social gospel seeks to bring men under repentance for their collective sins and to create a more sensitive and more modern conscience. It calls on us for the faith of the old prophets who believed in the salvation of nations.

Now, if this insight and religious outlook become common to large and vigorous sections of the Christian Church, the solutions of life contained in the old theological system will seem puny and inadequate. Our faith will be larger than the intellectual system which subtends it. Can theology expand to meet the growth of faith? The biblical studies have responded to the spiritual hunger aroused by the social gospel. The historical interpretation of the Bible has put the religious personalities, their spiritual struggles, their growth, and their utterances, into social connection with the community life of which they were part. This method of interpretation has given back the Bible to men of modernized intelligence and has made it the feeder of faith in the social gospel. The studies of "practical theology" are all in a process of rejuvenation and expansion in order to create competent leadership for the Church, and most of these changes are due to the rise of new ideals created by the social gospel. What, then, will doctrinal theology

[1] In his *Social Idealism and the Changing Theology*, embodying the Taylor Lectures for 1912, Gerald B. Smith has shown clearly the discrepancy created by the aristocratic attitude of authority in theology and the spread of democracy in modern ethical life, and has insisted that a readjustment is necessary in theology at this point to conform it to our ethical ideals. Professor Smith expresses the fear that our critical methods by themselves will lead only to a barren intellectualism. That feeling has been one motive in the writing of the present book.

do to meet the new situation? Can it ground and anchor the social gospel in the eternal truths of our religion and build its main ideas into the systematic structure of christian doctrine?

Theology is not superior to the gospel. It exists to aid the preaching of salvation. Its business is to make the essential facts and principles of Christianity so simple and clear, so adequate and mighty, that all who preach or teach the gospel, both ministers and laymen, can draw on its stores and deliver a complete and unclouded Christian message. When the progress of humanity creates new tasks, such as world-wide missions, or new problems, such as the social problem, theology must connect these with the old fundamentals of our faith and make them Christian tasks and problems.

The adjustment of the Christian message to the regeneration of the social order is plainly one of the most difficult tasks ever laid on the intellect of religious leaders. The pioneers of the social gospel have had a hard time trying to consolidate their old faith and their new aim. Some have lost their faith; others have come out of the struggle with crippled formulations of truth. Does not our traditional theology deserve some of the blame for this spiritual wastage because it left these men without spiritual support and allowed them to become the vicarious victims of our theological inefficiency? If our theology is silent on social salvation, we compel college men and women, workingmen, and theological students, to choose between an unsocial system of theology and an irreligious system of social salvation. It is not hard to predict the outcome. If we seek to keep Christian doctrine unchanged, we shall ensure its abandonment.

Instead of being an aid in the development of the social gospel, systematic theology has often been a real clog. When a minister speaks to his people about child labour or the exploitation of the lowly by the strong; when he insists on adequate food, education, recreation, and a really human opportunity for all, there is response. People are moved by plain human feeling and by the instinctive convictions which they have learned from Jesus Christ. But at once there are doubting and dissenting voices. We are told that environment has no saving power; regeneration is what men need; we can not have a regenerate society without regenerate individuals; we do not live for this world but for the life to come; it is not the function of the church to deal with economic questions; any effort to change the social order before the coming of the Lord is foredoomed to failure. These objections all issue from the theological consciousness created by traditional church teaching. These half-truths are the proper product of a halfway system of theology in which there is no room for social redemption. Thus the

Church is halting between two voices that call it. On the one side is the voice of the living Christ amid living men today; on the other side is the voice of past ages embodied in theology. Who will say that the authority of this voice has never confused our Christian judgment and paralysed our determination to establish God's Kingdom on earth?

Those who have gone through the struggle for a clear faith in the social gospel would probably agree that the doctrinal theology in which they were brought up, was one of the most baffling hindrances in their spiritual crisis, and that all their mental energies were taxed to overcome the weight of its traditions. They were fortunate if they promptly discovered some recent theological book which showed them at least the possibility of conceiving Christian doctrine in social terms, and made them conscious of a fellowship of faith in their climb toward the light. The situation would be much worse if Christian thought were nourished on doctrine only. Fortunately our hymns and prayers have a richer consciousness of solidarity than individualistic theology. But even today many ministers have a kind of dumb-bell system of thought, with the social gospel at one end and individual salvation at the other end, and an attenuated connection between them. The strength of our faith is in its unity. Religion wants wholeness of life. We need a rounded system of doctrine large enough to take in all our spiritual interests.

In short, we need a theology large enough to contain the social gospel, and alive and productive enough not to hamper it.

*

THE NATURE of Rauschenbusch's discussion may be better understood if brief reference is here made to certain chapters which for lack of space cannot be quoted here. The titles of Chapters II to XII, inclusive, are: "The Difficulties of Theological Readjustment," "Neither Alien nor Novel," "The Consciousness of Sin," "The Fall of Man," "The Nature of Sin," "The Transmission of Sin," "The Super-Personal Forces of Evil," "The Kingdom of Evil," "The Social Gospel and Personal Salvation," "The Salvation of the Super-Personal Forces," "The Church as the Social Factor of Salvation."

Possibly especially pertinent, for one considering Rauschenbusch fifty years after his first important book in English, are the statements in Chapters VIII and IX on the corporate character of evil. In VIII, "The Super-Personal Forces of Evil," a brief, compact, and incisive one, Rauschenbusch held that the "individualistic theology has not trained the spiritual intelligence of Christian men and women to recognize and observe spiritual entities beyond the individual." Josiah Royce in his Problem of Christianity had clearly written that the human world consisted of two important levels "of mental beings—namely the beings that we usually call individuals and the beings that we call communities." A community was thus vastly more than an aggregation of individuals.

"This conception is of great importance for the doctrine of sin," Rauschenbusch then wrote. All sorts of organized groups in our social life varied greatly "in moral quality," and were "potent" in imposing moral standards on their members. "These super-personal forces count in the moral world not only through their authority over their members, but through their influence in the general social life. They are the most powerful ethical forces in our communities."

Obviously "evil collective forces" are asserted. Righteous organizations face temptations. Organizations formed for good ends become corrupted, or small corrupt groups form within organizations of decent citizens. "The higher the institution, the worse it is when it goes wrong." Woodrow Wilson's broad indictment of the German government on April 2, 1917, was correct and just, but no doubt also applied to other governments "with few exceptions." "The social gospel realizes the importance and power of the super-personal forces in the community."

Chapter IX, also brief, was the last one on the "discussion of the doctrine of sin." Theologians had paid more attention to original sin than to sources of sin in "present-day life." They had obscured the great doctrine of the Kingdom of God. They had ignored the transmission of evil "through the channels of social tradition." They had not sufficiently noted the way organized groups had deadened the consciences of individuals (the theses of Chapter VIII). The super-personal forces might be redeemed and thus become "new spiritual factors of the highest significance."

"The solidaristic spiritual conceptions which have been discussed must all be kept in mind and seen together, in order to realize the power and scope of the doctrine to which they converge: the Kingdom of Evil."

The conception of a Kingdom of Evil was old, with many interpretations and popular conceptions of the Satanic kingdom. Rauschenbusch would drop popular superstitions, and concepts which made "drafts on our credulity." "Yet we ought to get a solidaristic and organic conception of the power and reality of evil in the world. The social gospel is the only influence which can renew the idea of the Kingdom of Evil in modern minds, because it alone has an adequate sense of solidarity, and a sufficient grasp of the historical and social realities of sin."

Rauschenbusch then quoted Albrecht Ritschl on the acceptance of both a social conception of sin and "its correlated ideas in the doctrine of salvation."

Other chapters not quoted are entitled "The Initiator of the Kingdom of God," "The Holy Spirit, Revelation, Inspiration, and Prophecy," "Baptism and the Lord's Supper," "Eschatology," "The Social Gospel and the Atonement."

*

THE KINGDOM OF GOD

IF THEOLOGY is to offer an adequate doctrinal basis for the social gospel, it must not only make room for the doctrine of the Kingdom of God, but give it a central place and revise all other doctrines so that they will articulate organically with it.

This doctrine is itself the social gospel. Without it, the idea of redeeming the social order will be but an annex to the orthodox conception of the scheme of salvation. It will love like a Negro servant family in a detached cabin back of the white man's house in the South. If this doctrine gets the place which has always been its legitimate right, the practical proclamation and application of social morality will have a firm footing.

To those whose minds live in the social gospel, the Kingdom of God is a dear truth, the marrow of the gospel, just as the incarnation was to Athanasius, justification by faith alone to Luther, and the sovereignty of God to Jonathan Edwards. It was just as dear to Jesus. He too lived in it, and from it looked out on the world and the work he had to do.

Jesus always spoke of the Kingdom of God. Only two of his reported sayings contain the word "Church," and both passages are of questionable authenticity. It is safe to say that he never thought of founding the kind of institution which afterward claimed to be acting for him.

Yet immediately after his death, groups of disciples joined and consolidated by inward necessity. Each local group knew that it was part of a divinely founded fellowship mysteriously spreading through humanity, and awaiting the return of the Lord and the establishing of his Kingdom. This universal Church was loved with the same religious faith and reverence with which Jesus had loved the Kingdom of God. It was the partial and earthly realization of the divine Society, and at the Parousia the Church and the Kingdom would merge.

But the Kingdom was merely a hope, the Church a present reality.

The chief interest and affection flowed toward the Church. Soon, through a combination of causes, the name and idea of "the Kingdom" began to be displaced by the name and idea of "the Church" in the preaching, literature, and theological thought of the Church. Augustine completed this process in his *De Civitate Dei*. The Kingdom of God which has, throughout human history, opposed the Kingdom of Sin, is today embodied in the Church. The millennium began when the Church was founded. This practically substituted the actual, not the ideal Church for the Kingdom of God. The beloved ideal of Jesus became a vague phrase which kept intruding from the New Testament. Like Cinderella in the kitchen, it saw the other great dogmas furbished up for the ball, but no prince of theology restored it to its rightful place. The Reformation, too, brought no renascence of the doctrine of the Kingdom; it had only eschatological value, or was defined in blurred phrases borrowed from the Church. The present revival of the Kingdom idea is due to the combined influence of the historical study of the Bible and of the social gospel.

When the doctrine of the Kingdom of God shriveled to an undeveloped and pathetic remnant in Christian thought, this loss was bound to have far-reaching consequences. We are told that the loss of a single tooth from the arch of the mouth in childhood may spoil the symmetrical development of the skull and produce malformations affecting the mind and character. The atrophy of that idea which had occupied the chief place in the mind of Jesus, necessarily affected the conception of Christianity, the life of the Church, the progress of humanity, and the structure of theology. I shall briefly enumerate some of the consequences affecting theology. This list, however, is by no means complete.

1. Theology lost its contact with the synoptic thought of Jesus. Its problems were not at all the same which had occupied his mind. It lost his point of view and became to some extent incapable of understanding him. His ideas had to be rediscovered in our time. Traditional theology and the mind of Jesus Christ became incommensurable quantities. It claimed to regard his revelation and the substance of his thought as divine, and yet did not learn to think like him. The loss of the Kingdom idea is one key to this situation.

2. The distinctive ethical principles of Jesus were the direct outgrowth of his conception of the Kingdom of God. When the latter disappeared from theology, the former disappeared from ethics. Only persons having the substance of the Kingdom ideal in their minds, seem to be able to get relish out of the ethics of Jesus. Only those church bodies which have been in opposition to organized society and have

looked for a better city with its foundations in heaven, have taken the Sermon on the Mount seriously.

3. The Church is primarily a fellowship for worship; the Kingdom is a fellowship of righteousness. When the latter was neglected in theology, the ethical force of Christianity was weakened; when the former was emphasized in theology, the importance of worship was exaggerated. The prophets and Jesus had cried down sacrifices and ceremonial performances, and cried up righteousness, mercy, solidarity. Theology now reversed this, and by its theoretical discussions did its best to stimulate sacramental actions and priestly importance. Thus the religious energy and enthusiasm which might have saved mankind from its great sins, were used up in hearing and endowing masses, or in maintaining competitive church organizations, while mankind is still stuck in the mud. There are nations in which the ethical condition of the masses is the reverse of the frequency of the masses in the churches.

4. When the Kingdom ceased to be the dominating religious reality, the Church moved up into the position of the supreme good. To promote the power of the Church and its control over all rival political forces was equivalent to promoting the supreme ends of Christianity. This increased the arrogance of churchmen and took the moral check off their policies. For the Kingdom of God can never be promoted by lies, craft, crime or war, but the wealth and power of the Church have often been promoted by these means. The medieval ideal of the supremacy of the Church over the State was the logical consequence of making the Church the highest good with no superior ethical standard by which to test it. The medieval doctrines concerning the Church and the Papacy were the direct theological outcome of the struggles for Church supremacy, and were meant to be weapons in that struggle.

5. The Kingdom ideal is the test and corrective of the influence of the Church. When the Kingdom ideal disappeared, the conscience of the Church was muffled. It became possible for the missionary expansion of Christianity to halt for centuries without creating any sense of shortcoming. It became possible for the most unjust social conditions to fasten themselves on Christian nations without awakening any consciousness that the purpose of Christ was being defied and beaten back. The practical undertakings of the Church remained within narrow lines, and the theological thought of the Church was necessarily confined in a similar way. The claims of the Church were allowed to stand in theology with no conditions and obligations to test and balance them. If the Kingdom had stood as the purpose for which the Church exists, the Church could not have fallen into such corruption and sloth. Theology

bears part of the guilt for the pride, the greed, and the ambition of the Church.

6. The Kingdom ideal contains the revolutionary force of Christianity. When this ideal faded out of the systematic thought of the Church, it became a conservative social influence and increased the weight of the other stationary forces in society. If the Kingdom of God had remained part of the theological and Christian consciousness, the Church could not, down to our times, have been salaried by autocratic class governments to keep the democratic and economic impulses of the people under check.

7. Reversely, the movements for democracy and social justice were left without a religious backing for lack of the Kingdom idea. The Kingdom of God as the fellowship of righteousness, would be advanced by the abolition of industrial slavery and the disappearance of the slums of civilization; the Church would only indirectly gain through such social changes. Even today many Christians can not see any religious importance in social justice and fraternity because it does not increase the number of conversions nor fill the churches. Thus the practical conception of salvation, which is the effective theology of the common man and minister, has been cut back and crippled for lack of the Kingdom ideal.

8. Secular life is belittled as compared with church life. Services rendered to the Church get a higher religious rating than services rendered to the community.[1] Thus the religious value is taken out of the activities of the common man and the prophetic services to society. Wherever the Kingdom of God is a living reality in Christian thought, any advance of social righteousness is seen as a part of redemption and arouses inward joy and the triumphant sense of salvation. When the Church absorbs interest, a subtle asceticism creeps back into our theology and the world looks different.

9. When the doctrine of the Kingdom of God is lacking in theology, the salvation of the individual is seen in its relation to the Church and to the future life, but not in its relation to the task of saving the social order. Theology has left this important point in a condition so hazy and muddled that it has taken us almost a generation to see that the salvation of the individual and the redemption of the social order are closely related, and how.

10. Finally, theology has been deprived of the inspiration of great ideas contained in the idea of the Kingdom and in labor for it. The

---

[1] After the death of Susan B. Anthony a minister commented on her life, regretting that she was not orthodox in her beliefs. In the same address he spoke glowingly about a new linoleum laid in the church kitchen.

Kingdom of God breeds prophets; the Church breeds priests and theologians. The Church runs to tradition and dogma; the Kingdom of God rejoices in forecasts and boundless horizons. The men who have contributed the most fruitful impulses to Christian thought have been men of prophetic vision, and their theology has proved most effective for future times where it has been most concerned with past history, with present social problems, and with the future of human society. The Kingdom of God is to theology what outdoor color and light are to art. It is impossible to estimate what inspirational impulses have been lost to theology and to the Church, because it did not develop the doctrine of the Kingdom of God and see the world and its redemption from that point of view.

These are some of the historical effects which the loss of the doctrine of the Kingdom of God has inflicted on systematic theology. The chief contribution which the social gospel has made and will make to theology is to give new vitality and importance to that doctrine. In doing so it will be a reformatory force of the highest importance in the field of doctrinal theology, for any systematic conception of Christianity must be not only defective but incorrect if the idea of the Kingdom of God does not govern it.

The restoration of the doctrine of the Kingdom has already made progress. Some of the ablest and most voluminous works of the old theology in their thousands of pages gave the Kingdom of God but a scanty mention, usually in connection with eschatology, and saw no connection between it and the Calvinistic doctrines of personal redemption. The newer manuals not only make constant reference to it in connection with various doctrines, but they arrange their entire subject matter so that the Kingdom of God becomes the governing idea.[2]

[2] William Adams Brown, *Christian Theology in Outline*, 192: "We are witnessing to-day a reaction against this exaggerated individualism (of Reformation theology). It has become an axiom of modern thought that the government of God has social as well as individual significance, and the conception of the Kingdom of God—obscured in the earlier Protestantism—is coming again into the forefront of theological thought." See the discussion on "The View of the Kingdom in Modern Thought" which follows.

Albrecht Ritschl, in his great monograph on Justification and Reconciliation, begins the discussion of his own views in Vol. III (§ 2) by insisting that personal salvation must be organically connected with the Kingdom of God. He says (*Rechtfertigung und Versöhnung*, III, III): "Theology has taken a very unequal interest in the two chief characteristics of Christianity. Everything pertaining to its character as the redemption of men has been made the subject of the most minute consideration; consequently redemption by Christ has been taken as the centre of all Christian knowledge and life, whereas the ethical conception of Christianity contained in the idea of the Kingdom of God has been slighted. . . . It has been fatal for Protestantism that

In the following brief propositions I should like to offer a few suggestions, on behalf of the social gospel, for the theological formulation of the doctrine of the Kingdom. Something like this is needed to give us "a theology for the social gospel."

1. The Kingdom of God is divine in its origin, progress, and consummation. It was initiated by Jesus Christ, in whom the prophetic spirit came to its consummation, it is sustained by the Holy Spirit, and it will be brought to its fulfillment by the power of God in his own time. The passive and active resistance of the Kingdom of Evil at every stage of its advance is so great, and the human resources of the Kingdom of God so slender, that no explanation can satisfy a religious mind which does not see the power of God in its movements. The Kingdom of God, therefore, is miraculous all the way, and is the continuous revelation of the power, the righteousness, and the love of God. The establishment of a community of righteousness in mankind is just as much a saving act of God as the salvation of an individual from his natural selfishness and moral inability. The Kingdom of God, therefore, is not merely ethical, but has a rightful place in theology. This doctrine is absolutely necessary to establish that organic union between religion and morality, between theology and ethics, which is one of the characteristics of the Christian religion. When our moral actions are consciously related to the Kingdom of God they gain religious quality. Without this doctrine we shall have expositions of schemes of redemption and we shall have systems of ethics, but we shall not have a true exposition of Christianity. The first step to the reform of the Churches is the restoration of the doctrine of the Kingdom of God.

2. The Kingdom of God contains the teleology of the Christian religion. It translates theology from the static to the dynamic. It sees, not doctrines or rites to be conserved and perpetuated, but resistance to be overcome and great ends to be achieved. Since the Kingdom of God is the supreme purpose of God, we shall understand the Kingdom so far as we understand God, and we shall understand God so far as we understand his Kingdom. As long as organized sin is in the world, the Kingdom of God is characterized by conflict with evil. But if there were

the Reformers did not cleanse the idea of the ethical Kingdom of God or Christ from its hierarchical corruption (i.e., the idea that the visible Church is identical with the Kingdom), but worked out the idea only in an academic and unpractical form." Kant first recognized the importance of the Kingdom of God for ethics. Schleiermacher first applied the teleological quality of Christianity to the definition of its nature, but he still treated now of personal redemption and now of the Kingdom of God, without adequately working out their connection. Ritschl has done more than any one else to put the idea to the front in German theology, but he does not get beyond a few great general ideas. He was born too early to get sociological ideas.

no evil, or after evil has been overcome, the Kingdom of God will still be the end to which God is lifting the race. It is realized not only by redemption, but also by the education of mankind and the revelation of his life within it.

3. Since God is in it, the Kingdom of God is always both present and future. Like God it is in all tenses, eternal in the midst of time. It is the energy of God realizing itself in human life. Its future lies among the mysteries of God. It invites and justifies prophecy, but all prophecy is fallible; it is valuable in so far as it grows out of action for the Kingdom and impels action. No theories about the future of the Kingdom of God are likely to be valuable or true which paralyze or postpone redemptive action on our part. To those who postpone, it is a theory and not a reality. It is for us to see the Kingdom of God as always coming, always pressing in on the present, always big with possibility, and always inviting immediate action. We walk by faith. Every human life is so placed that it can share with God in the creation of the Kingdom, or can resist and retard its progress. The Kingdom is for each of us the supreme task and the supreme gift of God. By accepting it as a task, we experience it as a gift. By laboring for it we enter into the joy and peace of the Kingdom as our divine fatherland and habitation.

4. Even before Christ, men of God saw the Kingdom of God as the great end to which all divine leadings were pointing. Every idealistic interpretation of the world, religious or philosophical, needs some such conception. Within the Christian religion the idea of the Kingdom gets its distinctive interpretation from Christ. (a) Jesus emancipated the idea of the Kingdom from previous nationalistic limitations and from the debasement of lower religious tendencies, and made it world-wide and spiritual. (b) He made the purpose of salvation essential in it. (c) He imposed his own mind, his personality, his love and holy will on the idea of the Kingdom. (d) He not only foretold it but initiated it by his life and work. As humanity more and more develops a racial consciousness in modern life, idealistic interpretations of the destiny of humanity will become more influential and important. Unless theology has a solidaristic vision higher and fuller than any other, it cannot maintain the spiritual leadership of mankind, but will be outdistanced. Its business is to infuse the distinctive qualities of Jesus Christ into its teachings about the Kingdom, and this will be a fresh competitive test of his continued headship of humanity.

5. The Kingdom of God is humanity organized according to the will of God. Interpreting it through the consciousness of Jesus we may affirm these convictions about the ethical relations within the Kingdom: (a)

Since Christ revealed the divine worth of life and personality, and since his salvation seeks the restoration and fulfillment of even the least, it follows that the Kingdom of God, at every stage of human development, tends toward a social order which will best guarantee to all personalities their freest and highest development. This involves the redemption of social life from the cramping influence of religious bigotry, from the repression of self-assertion in the relation of upper and lower classes, and from all forms of slavery in which human beings are treated as mere means to serve the ends of others. (b) Since love is the supreme law of Christ, the Kingdom of God implies a progressive reign of love in human affairs. We can see its advance wherever the free will of love supersedes the use of force and legal coercion as a regulative of the social order. This involves the redemption of society from political autocracies and economic oligarchies; the substitution of redemptive for vindictive penology; the abolition of constraint through hunger as part of the industrial system; and the abolition of war as the supreme expression of hate and the completest cessation of freedom. (c) The highest expression of love is the free surrender of what is truly our own, life, property, and rights. A much lower but perhaps more decisive expression of love is the surrender of any opportunity to exploit men. No social group or organization can claim to be clearly within the Kingdom of God which drains others for its own ease, and resists the effort to abate this fundamental evil. This involves the redemption of society from private property in the natural resources of the earth, and from any condition in industry which makes monopoly profits possible. (d) The reign of love tends toward the progressive unity of mankind, but with the maintenance of individual liberty and the opportunity of nations to work out their own national peculiarities and ideals.

6. Since the Kingdom is the supreme end of God, it must be the purpose for which the Church exists. The measure in which it fulfills this purpose is also the measure of its spiritual authority and honor. The institutions of the Church, its activities, its worship, and its theology must in the long run be tested by its effectiveness in creating the Kingdom of God. For the Church to see itself apart from the Kingdom, and to find its aims in itself, is the same sin of selfish detachment as when an individual selfishly separates himself from the common good. The Church has the power to save in so far as the Kingdom of God is present in it. If the Church is not living for the Kingdom, its institutions are part of the "world." In that case it is not the power of redemption but its object. It may even become an anti-Christian power. If any form of church organization which formerly aided the Kingdom now impedes it, the reason for its existence is gone.

7. Since the Kingdom is the supreme end, all problems of personal salvation must be reconsidered from the point of view of the Kingdom. It is not sufficient to set the two aims of Christianity side by side. There must be a synthesis, and theology must explain how the two react on each other. (Noted in an earlier chapter.) The entire redemptive work of Christ must also be reconsidered under this orientation. Early Greek theology saw salvation chiefly as the redemption from ignorance by the revelation of God and from earthliness by the impartation of immortality. It interpreted the work of Christ accordingly, and laid stress on his incarnation and resurrection. Western theology saw salvation mainly as forgiveness of guilt and freedom from punishment. It interpreted the work of Christ accordingly, and laid stress on the death and atonement. If the Kingdom of God was the guiding idea and chief end of Jesus—as we now know it was—we may be sure that every step in His life, including His death, was related to that aim and its realization, and when the idea of the Kingdom of God takes its due place in theology, the work of Christ will have to be interpreted afresh.

8. The Kingdom of God is not confined within the limits of the Church and its activities. It embraces the whole of human life. It is the Christian transfiguration of the social order. The Church is one social institution alongside of the family, the industrial organization of society, and the state. The Kingdom of God is in all these, and realizes itself through them all. During the Middle Ages all society was ruled and guided by the Church. Few of us would want modern life to return to such a condition. Functions which the Church used to perform, have now far outgrown its capacities. The Church is indispensable to the religious education of humanity and to the conservation of religion, but the greatest future awaits religion in the public life of humanity.

*

THE SOCIAL GOSPEL AND THE
CONCEPTION OF GOD

MY MAIN purpose in this book has been to show that the social gospel is a vital part of the Christian conception of sin and salvation, and that any teaching on the sinful condition of the race and on its redemption from evil which fails to do justice to the social factors and processes in sin and redemption, must be incomplete, unreal, and misleading. Also, since the social gospel henceforth is to be an important part of our Christian message, its chief convictions must be embodied in these doctrines in some organic form.

The conception of God held by a social group is a social product. Even if it originated in the mind of a solitary thinker or prophet, as soon as it becomes the property of a social group, it takes on the qualities of that group. If, for instance, a high and spiritual idea of God is brought to a people ignorant and accustomed to superstitious methods of winning the favor or help of highest beings, it will soon be coarsened and materialized. The changes in the Hebrew conception of God were the result of the historical experiences of the nation and its leaders. The Christian idea of God has also had its ups and downs in the long and varied history of Christian civilization.

A fine and high conception of God is a social achievement and a social endowment. It becomes part of the spiritual inheritance common to all individuals in that religious group. If every individual had to work out his idea of God on the basis of his own experiences and intuitions only, it would be a groping quest, and most of us would see only the occasional flitting of a distant light. By the end of our life we might have arrived at the stage of voodooism or necromancy. Entering into a high conception of God, such as the Christian faith offers us, is like entering a public park or a public gallery of art and sharing the common wealth. When we learn from the gospels, for instance, that God is on the side of the poor, and that he proposes to view anything done or not done to them as having been done or not done to him, such a revelation of solidarity and humanity comes with a regenerating shock to our selfish minds. Any one studying life as it is on the basis of real estate and bank clearings, would come to the conclusion that God is on the side of the rich. It takes a revelation to see it the other way.

Wherever we encounter such a strain of social feeling in our conceptions of God, it is almost sure to run straight back either to Jesus or the prophets. The Hebrew prophets were able to realize God in that way because they were part of a nation which had preserved the traditions of primitive fraternal democracy. The prophets emphasized God's interest in righteousness and solidarity because they were making a fight to save their people from the landlordism and oppression under which other peoples have wilted and degenerated. When, therefore, we today feel the moral thrill of Hebrew theism, we are the heirs and beneficiaries of one untamed nation of mountain dwellers. When such a conception of God is transmitted to other nations or to later times, it is the exportation of the most precious commodity a nation can produce.

On the other hand, if a conception of God originates among the exploiting classes in an age of despotism, it is almost certain to contain germs of positive sinfulness which will infect all to whom it is transmitted.

Thus the social relations in which men lived, affected their conceptions about God and his relations to men. Under tyrannous conditions the idea of God was necessarily tainted with the cruel hardness of society. This spiritual influence of despotism made even the face of Christ seem hard and stern. The outlook into the future life was like a glimpse into a chamber of torture.

The value of the Reformation should be reassessed. Luther tore the idea of "merit" out of theology. Christ alone had merit. By his blood he had paid the whole debt once for all. Man need not earn merit. He can not earn merit. It would be a sin for him to try. That ended the contract labor system in religion. God was reconciled. He had been angry but he was now kind and ready to forgive. The sinner need only believe and accept the great transaction made on his behalf. That ended the reign of fear for those who understood. The saints and their intercession were dismissed; they never had any merit either; the sinner could deal with God and Christ direct. Purgatory was gone; only hell proper remained. It was a religious Seisachtheia, like that in Athens under Solon's laws, a great unloading, a revolution in the field of the spiritual life, and the condition for the coming of political and economic liberty.

But the restoration of the Christian conception of God was by no means complete. Despotic government was still in full swing when the Reformation theology was written. Luther and Calvin were not personally in sympathy with democracy. The age of absolutism and of Louis XIV was just ahead. The long era of witch trials had just begun. The spell of fear was broken only for a few. The fundamental assumptions about God remained. The inherited forensic terminology of theology suggested the old lines of thought. As long as religion borrows its terms from the procedure of law courts, the spirit of coercion and terror leaks in. Legal ideas are not congruous with the Christian consciousness of salvation. The idea of "justification" did not come to us from Jesus and it does not blend well with his way of thinking. For Paul and Luther "justification by faith" was an emancipating idea; it stood for an immense simplification and sweetening of the process of salvation. They used the terminology of legalism to deny its spirit. To us, who are not under the consciousness of Jewish or Roman Catholic legality, "justification" does not convey the same sense of liberation, but the phrase is now a vehicle by which legal and often despotic ideas come back to plague us.

The social gospel is God's predestined agent to continue what the

Reformation began. It arouses intelligent hatred of oppression and the reign of fear, and teaches us to prize liberty and to love love. Therefore those whose religious life has been influenced by the social gospel are instinctively out of sympathy with autocratic conceptions of God. They sense the spiritual taint which goes out from such ideas. They know that these religious conceptions are used to make autocratic social conditions look tolerable, necessary, and desirable. Like Paul, the social gospel has not "received the spirit of bondage again unto fear." It is wholly in sympathy with the conception of the Father which Jesus revealed to us by his words, by his personality, and by his own relations to the Father.

This reformatory and democratizing influence of the social gospel is not against religion but for it. The worst thing that could happen to God would be to remain an autocrat while the world is moving toward democracy. He would be dethroned with the rest. For one man who has forsaken religion through scientific doubt, ten have forsaken it in our time because it seemed the spiritual opponent of liberty and the working people. This feeling will deepen as democracy takes hold and becomes more than a theory of government. We have heard only the political overture of democracy, played by fifes; the economic numbers of the program are yet to come, and they will be performed with trumpets and trombones.

The Kingdom of God is the necessary background for the Christian idea of God. The social movement is one of the chief ways in which God is revealing that he lives and rules as a God that loves righteousness and hates iniquity. A theological God who has no interest in the conquest of justice and fraternity is not a Christian. It is not enough for theology to eliminate this or that autocratic trait. Its God must join the social movement. The real God has been in it long ago. The development of a Christian social order would be the highest proof of God's saving power. The failure of the social movement would impugn his existence.

The old conception that God dwells on high and is distinct from our human life was the natural basis for autocratic and arbitrary ideas about him. On the other hand the religious belief that he is immanent in humanity is the natural basis for democratic ideas about him. When he was far above, he needed vicegerents to rule for him, popes by divine institution and kings by divine right. If he lives and moves in the life of mankind, he can act directly on the masses of men. A God who strives within our striving, who kindles his flame in our intellect, sends the impact of his energy to make our will restless for righteousness, floods our subconscious mind with dreams and longings, and always urges the race on toward a higher combination of freedom and solidarity —that would be a God with whom democratic and religious men could hold converse as their chief fellow worker, the source of their energies, the ground of their hopes.

Platonic philosophy in the first century made God so transcendent that it had to devise the Logos idea to bridge the abyss between the silent depths of God and this world, and to enable God to create and to reveal himself. Theology shrank from imputing suffering to God. Patripassianism seemed a self-evident heresy. Today men want to think of God as close to them, and spiritually kin to them, the Father of all spirits. Eminent theologians insist that God has always suffered with and for mankind and that the cross is a permanent law of God's nature: "The lamb has been slain from the beginning of the world." Through the conception of evolution and through the social movement we have come to see human life in its totality, and our consciousness of God is the spiritual counterpart of our social consciousness. Some, apparently, would be willing to think of God as less than omnipotent and omniscient if only he were working hard with us for that Kingdom which is the only true Democracy.

Two points still demand discussion. The first is the problem of suffering.

The existence of innocent suffering impugns the justice and benevolence of God, both of which are essential in a Christian conception of God.

The simplest solution is to deny the existence of unjust suffering; to trust that good and ill are allotted according to desert; and if the righteous Job suffers great disaster, to search for his secret sin. This explanation broke down before the facts. How about the man born blind? What personal sin had merited his calamity?

Dualism took the other extreme. It acknowledged that the good suffer, and stressed the fact. But it exculpated the good God by making the evil God the author of this world, or at least its present lord.

Christianity has combined several explanations of suffering. It grounds it in general on the prevalence of sin since the fall. It has ascribed a malignant power of afflicting the righteous to Satan and his servants. It has taken satisfaction when justice was vindicated in some striking case of goodness or wickedness. It has held out a hope of a public vindication of the righteous in the great judgment, and of an equalization of their lot by their bliss in heaven and the suffering of the wicked. (This element, however, was weakened in Protestantism by the disappearance of purgatory and the tacit assumption that all who are saved at all will enjoy an equal bliss. Purgatory was a great balancer and equalizer.) Finally, Christianity has taught that God allots suffering with wise and loving intent, tempering it according to our strength, relieving it in response to our prayer, and using it to chasten our pride, to win us from earthliness to himself, and to prepare us for heaven. This interpretation does not assert the justice of every suffering, taken by itself, but does maintain its loving intention.

All these are powerful and comforting considerations. But they are shaken by the bulk of the unjust suffering in sight of the modern mind. These Christian ideas are largely true as long as we look at a normal village community and its individuals and families. But they are jarred by mass disasters. The optimism of the age of rationalism was shaken by the Lisbon earthquake in 1755, when thirty thousand people were killed together, just and unjust. The War has deeply affected the religious assurance of our own time, and will lessen it still more when the excitement is over and the aftermath of innocent suffering becomes clear. But that impression of undeserved mass misery which the War has brought home to the thoughtless, has long been weighing on all who understood the social conditions of our civilization. The sufferings of a single righteous man could deeply move the psalmists or the poet of Job. Today entire social classes sit in the ashes and challenge the justice of the God who has afflicted them by fathering the present social system. The moral and religious problem of suffering has entered on a new stage with the awakening of the social consciousness and the spread of social knowledge.

If God stands for the present social order, how can we defend him? We can stand the pain of travail, of physical dissolution, of earthquakes and accidents. These are the price we pay for the use of a fine planet with lovely appurtenances and for a wonderful body. We can also accept with reasonable resignation the mental anguish of unrequited love, of foiled ambition, or of the emptiness of life. These are the risks we run as possessors of a highly organized personality amid a world of men. But we can not stand for poor and laborious people being deprived of physical stature, youth, education, human equality, and justice, in order to enable others to live luxurious lives. It revolts us to see these conditions perpetuated by law and organized force, and palliated or justified by the makers of public opinion. None of the keys offered by individualistic Christianity fit this padlock..

The social gospel supplies an explanation of this class of human suffering. Society is so integral that when one man sins, other men suffer, and when one social class sins, the other classes are involved in the suffering which follows on that sin. The more powerful an individual is, the more will he involve others; the more powerful a class is, the more will it be able to unload its own just suffering on the weaker classes. These sufferings are not "vicarious"; they are solidaristic.

Our solidarity is a beneficent part of human life. It is the basis for our greatest good. If our community life is righteous and fraternal, we are enriched and enlarged by being bound up with it. But, by the same law, if our community is organized in a way that permits, encourages, or defends predatory practices, then the larger part of its members are through solidarity caged to be eaten by the rest, and to suffer what is both unjust and useless.

It follows that ethically it is of the highest importance to prevent our beneficent solidarity from being twisted into a means of torture.

Physical pain serves a beneficent purpose by warning us of the existence of abnormal conditions. It fulfills its purpose when it compels the individual to search out the cause of pain and to keep his body in health. If he takes "dope" to quiet the consciousness of pain without healing the causes, the beneficent purpose of pain is frustrated.

Social suffering serves social healing. If the sense of common humanity is strong enough to set the entire social body in motion on behalf of those who suffer without just cause, then their troubles are eased and the whole body is preserved just and fraternal. If the predatory forces are strong enough to suppress the reactions against injustice and inhumanity, the suffering goes on and the whole community is kept in suicidal evil. To interpret the sufferings imposed by social injustice in individualistic terms as the divine chastening and sanctification of all the individuals concerned, is not only false but profoundly mischievous. It is the equivalent of "dope," for it silences the warning which the suffering of an innocent group ought to convey to all society without abolishing the causes. It frustrates the only chance of redemptive usefulness which the sufferers had.

All this applies to our conception of God. The idea of solidarity, when once understood, acts as a theodicy. None of us would want a world without organic community of life, any more than we would want a world without gravitation. The fact that a careless boy falls down stairs does not condemn gravitation, nor does the existence of evil community life condemn God who constituted us social beings. The innocent suffering of great groups through social solidarity simply brings home to us that the tolerance of social injustice is an intolerable evil. The great sin of men is to resist the reformation of predatory society. We do not want God to be charged with that attitude. A conception of God which describes him as sanctioning the present social order and utilizing it in order to sanctify its victims through their suffering, without striving for its overthrow, is repugnant to our moral sense. Both the Old Testament and the New Testament characterizations of God's righteousness assure us that he hates with steadfast hatred just such practices as modern communities tolerate and promote. If we can trust the Bible, God is against capitalism, its methods, spirit, and results. The bourgeois theologians have misrepresented our revolutionary God. God is for the Kingdom of God, and his Kingdom does not mean injustice and the perpetuation of innocent suffering. The best theodicy for modern needs is to make this very clear.

Finally, the social gospel emphasizes the fact that God is the bond of racial unity.

Speaking historically, it is one of the most universal and important characteristics of religion that it constitutes the spiritual bond of social groups. A national god was always the exponent of national solidarity. A common religion created common sympathies. Full moral obligation stopped at the religious boundary line. The unusual thing about the Good Samaritan was that he disregarded the religious cleavage and followed the call of humanity pure and simple.

The mingling of populations and religions in modern life makes the influence of religion less noticeable, but it still works as a bond of sympathy. It is easiest to trace it where the religious cleavage coincides with the racial or political cleavages. The French Catholics in Quebec and the English Protestants in Ontario; the Irish and the Ulstermen; the Catholic Belgians and the Protestant Dutch; the Latin nations of America and the United States—the mention of the names brings up the problem. The Balkans are a nest of antagonisms partly because of religious differences. It has been fortunate for the American Negro that the antagonism of race and social standing has not been intensified in his case by any difference of religion.[1]

The spread of a monotheistic faith and the recognition of a single God of all mankind is a condition of an ethical union of mankind in the future. This is one of the long-range social effects of Christian missions. The effects of Christianity will go far beyond its immediate converts. Every competing religion will be compelled to emphasize its monotheistic elements and to allow its polytheistic ingredients to drop to a secondary stage.

But it is essential to our spiritual honesty that no imperialism shall

[1] I have seen Southern pamphlets undertaking to prove that the Negroes are not descended from Adam, but have evolved from African jungle beasts. The very orthodox authors were willing to accept the heretical philosophy of evolution for the black people, though of course they claimed biblical creation for the white. The purpose of this religious maneuvre is to cut the bond of human obligation and solidarity established by religion, and put the Negroes outside the protection of the moral law.

masquerade under the cover of our religion. Those who adopt the white man's religion come under the white man's influence. Christianity is the religion of the dominant race. The native religions are a spiritual bulwark of defence, independence, and loyalty. If we invite men to come under the same spiritual roof of monotheism with us and to abandon their ancient shelters, let us make sure that this will not be exploited as a trick of subjugation by the empires. As long as there are great colonizing imperialisms in the world, the propaganda of Christianity has a political significance.

God is the common basis of all our life. Our human personalities may seem distinct, but their roots run down into the eternal life of God. In a large way both philosophy and science are tending toward a recognition of the truth which religion has felt and practised. The all-pervading life of God is the ground of the spiritual oneness of the race and of our hope for its closer fellowship in the future.

The consciousness of solidarity, therefore, is of the essence of religion. But the circumference and spaciousness of the fellowship within it differ widely. Every discovery of a larger fellowship by the individual brings a glow of religious satisfaction. The origin of the Christian religion was bound up with a great transition from a nationalistic to an international religious consciousness. Paul was the hero of that conquest. The Christian God has been a breaker of barriers from the first. All who have a distinctively Christian experience of God are committed to the expansion of human fellowship and to the overthrow of barriers. To emphasize this and bring it home to the Christian consciousness is part of the mission of the social gospel, and it looks to theology for the intellectual formulation of what it needs.

We have discussed three points in this chapter: how the conception of God can be cleansed from the historic accretions of despotism and be democratized; how it can be saved from the indictment contained in the unjust suffering of great social groups; and how we can realize God as the ground of social unity. Freedom, justice, solidarity are among the aims of the social gospel.

* VIII *

Contributions to the Baptist Congress

B ETWEEN 1889 and 1908 Rauschenbusch made a number of formal and informal contributions in writing to the proceedings of the Baptist Congress. During most of this time he was the minister of the Second Baptist Church in New York. This was the period when his emphasis in reading changed from personal piety to the writings of economists, sociologists, reformers, and of those theologians aware of the social crises of the times.

In this era an influential figure was John Peter Altgeld, who influenced the social thought of both Bryan and Theodore Roosevelt. Altgeld, an immigrant from Germany, served in the Union army during the American Civil War. Later he taught school and studied law. He became a lawyer and a judge in Illinois, serving as governor of Illinois, 1893-97. When governor he pardoned the anarchists who had been imprisoned for participation in the Haymarket Riot, an act which resulted in a prolonged national controversy, and cost him his political future. But this was the flame which ignited social causes and burned on in such thinkers as Rauschenbusch.

The Baptist Congress for the discussion of current questions functioned from 1882 to 1913, with Rauschenbusch as an active participant and secretary for a large part of the time. The Congress brought together leaders from both the Northern Baptist Convention and the Southern Baptist Convention, in a forum for consideration of many important issues before both Church and State. Papers were presented on such issues as church polity and policy, the regulation of corporations by government, the relations of the churches and the government in America. It was customary to have one or more formal papers read before these sessions, held in cities both North and South, followed by comments. Proceedings were then published.

Rauschenbusch contributed boldly, both through formal papers and the discussions. His name also appears frequently in the proceedings on subject matter ranging from economics to Church-State relations and *the role of the pulpit in economic reform. A selection from this vigorous writing is here presented.*

✳

THE CHURCH AND MONEY POWER

A PAPER read, December 5, 1893, at the Baptist Congress for the discussion of current questions, Augusta, from which a large portion is here quoted:

What is the relation between the power exerted in the world by the Church of Christ and the power wielded by wealth? Do they run parallel or counter? Are they friends or enemies? If the latter, which of the two has triumphed in the struggle between them? Has the Church brought wealth into captivity to the spirit of Christ? Or has wealth corrupted the Church, warped it from its mission and made it subservient to the spirit of the world?

Perhaps we shall best do justice to these questions, if we first consider the nature of the Church and of money power; secondly, glance over the history of their relations; thirdly, examine the relations they sustain to each other today and in our own religious community; and finally, draw what lessons we can from this study.

And first, I hold that the Church and money power are not friends, but enemies, opposed to each other in the same sense in which God and the world are opposed to each other. For the Church is the incarnation of the Christ-spirit, and accumulated wealth is the incarnation of the world-spirit. The Church stands for giving; wealth stands for taking, else how could it be wealthy? The Church stands for bending down to the weak and lifting them up; wealth, on the whole, stands for climbing up above the weak. The Church stands for the sacrifice of self to others; wealth stands for the sacrifice of others to self. Wealth envelops men in an atmosphere of levity and frivolity, where earnestness cools down and high purposes ooze away; the Church seeks to envelop men in an atmosphere of large thoughts and strenuous aims. The Church is both a partial realization of the new society, in which God's will is done, and also the appointed instrument for the further realization of that new society in the world about it. It seeks to supplant this present world era by the world era to come; to abolish things as they are and substitute things as they should be.

On the other hand wealth is a product of the world as it is. It has everything to gain from keeping things as they are, and everything to lose from the very condition which the Church is set to bring into the world. Therefore wealth is timid of change, and its power has always been exerted to counteract and foil the Church when the Church has really been about its Master's business. Hence Jesus bids his disciples not to lay up treasures, because if they do, their hearts will almost infallibly be where their treasures are, and will lose the power of upward flight. Hence he reiterates that no man can unite the service of God with the service of Mammon; for the service of God is inseparable from justice, simplicity, and love; and the service of Mammon, that is, the pursuit of wealth, is inseparable from extortion, selfishness and a hardening of the heart. Hence Jesus says that it is next to impossible for a rich man to enter the Kingdom, for the Kingdom of God implies relations of justice and love; but who can acquire great wealth without offending against justice in some way? And who can remain rich in the midst of poverty and yet have the love of God abiding in him?

This, then, is the historical summary of the relations between the Church and money power; implacable antagonism between the money power and the Church, when the Church is alive, outspoken, daring, and faithful to its Master; compromise, respect, neutrality, or an interchange of support between the money power and the Church, when the Church is drugged into insensibility.

We pass on to examine our present condition; and here above all we need an unflinching eye and steadfast courage, not only if we are to say the truth, but if we are to see it at all.

Has the Church shaken off the fetters of the money power? Is it standing freely in the noble company of prophets and martyrs, and proving by its spirit the genuineness of its apostolic succession? There are a number of symptoms that give us pause, before giving our own religious community a clean bill of health.

1. The scarcity of teaching on wealth. Estimate the proportional bulk of teaching on property in the prophets and in the synoptic gospels, as compared with other moral questions; and then estimate similarly the proportion of teaching devoted to the same questions by the Church today, and see if they tally.

2. The timidity of teaching on wealth. Whenever scriptural passages on wealth have to be expounded, there is a noticeable softness of tread, a weighing of words, an air of apology. There is no such carefulness in dealing, for instance, with the drink question. We charge the Roman Church with timidity on that question because so many of its influential members are engaged in that traffic. Is it not possible that our timidity on covetousness is due to our having covetous men among us and being afraid of them?

3. The indefiniteness of our teaching. Our casuistry is vague. Compare the editorials of our denominational press on church polity or the terms of communion with the editorials on strikes and the labor movement. In the one case they make straight for their point and hit it hard when they get there. In the other case there is often a curious shunting off just before they get to the real outcome of the matter. There is no clear-cut set of opinions among us concerning questions of property. Why not?

4. The absence of church discipline for covetousness. Every live church would bar out a notoriously intemperate or licentious man, and if he profess conversion, there would be some more or less definite understanding, that those vices have been put away. Do we thus deal with men who are covetous, or are known to have been "close" all their lives? Do evangelists ever repeat the instructions which John the Baptist gave to his inquirer? Do preachers ever say approximately what Jesus said to the rich young ruler? And if any of our church members lapse into covetousness, do we exclude them? Who knows of a case of exclusion for covetousness? Yet there is clear and precise scriptural command to exclude them; three times as clear as for close communion. Why then do we not do it?

5. The influence of wealth in our church life. Wherever the contrast between rich and poor has had time to do its work, there are at first diverging classes inside of the same church. Next the rich gravitate to churches of their own; the rich and poor are separated; the body of Christ is rent asunder on lines of wealth, and the great heresy against the second Adam is an accomplished fact. Then in the wealthy churches the percentage of baptisms begins to decrease; they are recruited merely from the children of the members; real sacrifice becomes rare; the cross is cut out of Christianity; the aesthetic enjoyment of fine music, upholstery, and oratory takes the place of spirituality. Mammon has done his work.

6. The influence of wealth in our religious work. Though rich men are almost ruled out of the Kingdom of Jesus, and though rich churches are not the really spiritual churches, yet they wield an enormous power in the work of the church. The one rich man in the church often outweighs all the rest of the church. A junto of wealthy men have more than once ousted a pastor beloved by the rest of the church, or prevented the calling of a man who was known for outspoken preaching. Wealthy men preponderate on the boards of our religious organizations and often direct their affairs according to worldly prudence, in which they excel, rather than according to faith. In our New York City Mission Society one hundred church members are entitled to one voice; the

gift of one hundred dollars likewise entitles the giver to one voice. So that one hundred dollars weighs as much or more in the counsels of the society as one hundred Christian men and women.

7. The lack of leadership in movements for social righteousness. Wherever there is a movement to secure justice for the oppressed, the white standard of the Church of Jesus ought to wave far in advance of all others in the storming column. Future historians will record the latter half of the nineteenth century as the era of the great social movement. Is the Church leading in that movement? There are Christian individuals who lead. The general sentiment among ministers is very much on the side of the underdog. Yet the Church follows and does not lead. Take our own denominational press. I know of only one prominent Baptist paper which in a labor dispute is more ready to believe that the workingmen are right than that their employers are right, and is just as eager to record the success of a strike as the failure of one.

I have enumerated all these points as symptoms of our condition, because they indicate the present status of the contest between the Church and the money power. And if only half of my points are well taken, they prove, I think, that the struggle is not settled; that eternal vigilance is still the price of liberty; and that the Church is not pressing in the footsteps of the prophets and of Jesus, as it ought. Baptists have contended for the separation of Church and State. Why? Because they wanted to keep the Church free from the control of worldly men and their power, unbribed by their favors and unterrified by their hostility. The Church cannot fight the world, if it is in the world's pay. The irksome point of the union of Church and State for a godly minister in England was not his far-off relation to the government in London, but his dependence on the local nobleman by whose favor he obtained his living, who might be a worldly man, but who could nevertheless interfere in the work of the Church. That was union of the Church and State.

And is it not possible, with all our separation of Church and State in this country, for the Church to be under the control of worldly men still? Can they not present a minister to a church as much as an English lord, provided they are willing to contribute handsomely to the support of the church? Can they not influence the preaching of the minister? If I had in my audience a man who grinds his employees, but who contributes a fourth of my salary, could I talk freely about justice and mercy unless I had an unusual degree of Christian bravery? Should I be reading this paper now? Are we Baptists not under obligation to stand up against this informal and more insidious union of Church and State, as our fathers stood up against that form of the dependence of Christ on Mammon which fettered the Church in their day?

Finally, what can be done? What we pre-eminently need is fearless thinking and faithful preaching. There are still five brethren of Dives in the land of the living. Let us see that they get Moses and the prophets undiluted. We must cease to sing the half-true lullaby of consecrated wealth and stewardship, and tell men that they imperil their souls and decrease their usefulness by making money unjustly, and by hoarding it after they have it. We must create a new public opinion in the Christian community, which shall exercise a strong and unceasing pressure in the direction of justice and mercy, and shall be satisfied with no substitute for Christ's own code of ethics.

Especially we of the ministry, as teachers and leaders of our people, must set our faces like a flint against anything which will enslave the Church to the money power. It will mean less salary, an apparent loss of influence, dark looks, and many things that take the soul of a man near Gethsemane. But it will also mean fellowship with the Master and the joy and inward light which that gives. It will mean true and lasting service to the brethren, increasing wisdom, the faculty of leadership, and the affection of the best men in the world. It pays to "take no purse, no wallet, no shoes, and to salute no man on the way," in order to proclaim without let or hindrance the glad tidings to the poor. And, anyway, what has a servant of Jesus to do with the fear of man?

It would be especially important if those who engage in this conflict would stand together, uniting their counsels and their sympathy, supporting every man who bears hardship in the service of Jesus, and thus forming a new order of chivalry, the Knights of the Holy Ghost.

*

ETHICAL VERSUS FORENSIC CONCEPTIONS OF SALVATION

THIS was the theme of several papers read at the Baptist Congress for the discussion of current questions, Augusta, Georgia, December 6, 1893. The full text of the remarks following the papers is given here:

"Ethical versus Forensic Conceptions of Salvation"—what does it mean? I think it means this: Is it better to speak of salvation in terms borrowed from legal transactions, or in terms borrowed from the simpler relations of life in the family or in neighborly intercourse? In building our theories of religion, should we build them on those expressions of the Bible describing the relations between father and son, or those describing God as a judge and man as a condemned, pardoned, or justified criminal?

I want to make five points:

1. In speaking of the relations between God and man we must necessarily use terms borrowed from the relations between man and man. Our language has no other symbols, nor is our mind capable of conceiving anything else. "No man hath seen the Father." "If ye see me, ye see the Father." Whether we will or no, the only God we can think of or speak of, is a God with a human heart, and the more we try to evade that necessity, the more abstract and vague and cold will our God be.

2. But in the second place, these human terms, when applied to God and our relations to him, are symbols and only symbols. They approximate the real thing, but they are not identical with it. For instance, we hear of a man pardoned by the governor. "Ah," we say, "that is what God has done for me." Or we hear of a captive redeemed from slavery. "There," we say, "that is what God has done for me; he has freed me from the worst slavery of all." Or we hear of a wayward son who has been taken back by his father. We say: "God has been more forgiving to me than even that." So we take human experiences and relations, enlarge them and make them do service to express God's relations to us. But they are only symbols. Press them beyond a certain point and they become faulty and dangerous.

3. There are good symbols and bad symbols. To get the best symbols for God's ways, we must go to the best men. And in addition, we must take the life of the best men in those relations where their character finds the fullest and most rounded expression.

4. In general we may say that expressions taken from family life are preferable to those taken from court life. For a judge does not love a prisoner, usually, while God does love us. Hence conceptions of salvation expressed in the language of the courtroom are apt to leave out one of the most important sides of God's character, his love. Forensic conceptions are preferable to commercial conceptions, for the courts exist for justice, while commerce usually exists only for profit, which is one of the lowest things on earth, and its conceptions would be misleading if applied to God. But expressions borrowed from family life are better than legal expressions, because in the family justice and love are blended, and modify each other.

5. If forensic procedures are used to explain God's dealings with man, they should be the procedures of the noblest and most civilized courts on earth. We have all heard the story which is often told to illustrate

the atonement. In some country every person committing a certain offense was to have both his eyes put out. The king's son committed that offense, but the king, in his capacity as supreme judge, commanded that they take one eye from his son and one from himself, and it was so done. Now, that is a legal transaction which would not stand in any civilized court. It would arouse a cry of horror and protest in any decent community. If it ever happened, it happened in a barbaric nation. And when a theory concerning God's actions has to get its illustrations from barbarians, it condemns itself. If we want to know where God stands, we must find out where the best men stand, then draw a line through that point and prolong it to infinity and it will point in the direction of God. But we must not seek God in the direction of ethical practices which we ourselves have abandoned.

*

THE LESSONS OF ECONOMIC HISTORY

A LARGE portion of a paper, "State-help versus Self-help, or Pater- nalism in Government," read at the Baptist Congress for the dis- cussion of current questions, Buffalo, New York, November 16, 1898, follows:

We seek to draw the lessons of economic history. I shall try to sum- marize the experience of the past and the probable trend of the future in a few statements.

1. We shall never go back to unrestricted *laissez faire.* Evolutionary philosophy might permit. But we also have a heart educated by Chris- tianity, and a lively, though spasmodic, sense of human solidarity. It is not a question today whether we are to return to self-help, but whether we are to stop at state help or pass on to state ownership. The Duke of Argyll wisely says: "The two great discoveries of the present age in economic practice have been the desirability of removing restrictions on the free exchange of goods, and the absolute necessity of imposing conditions on the free disposal of labor."

2. It is no longer open to question that the state must interfere against the industrial exploitation of children, to safeguard their right to un- stunted physical growth and a fair measure of education.

3. Likewise the state must interfere on behalf of women. Experience has shown that women rarely organize in trade, and singly they are helpless. Moreover their case differs from that of men in that they do

not merely represent working capacity, but are the mothers of the race. When England declared it unfit that women work in mines, the usual objections were made both by mine owners and by the women; now everybody has acquiesced. But neither is it fit that young girls be kept standing all day in retail stores and enter marriage physically broken. Nor is it fit that nursing mothers work in factories while their babies are fed on artificial food at home, to die early or grow up puny.

4. The state must look after the sanitary condition of all places where larger numbers of people work together. It must regulate the air space, ventilation, heating, length of working time, meal hours, etc., in factories and stores. In our present huge organization of labor, in the shifting character of our working population, and in the absence of social bonds between employers and employees, these matters cannot be left to private contract. There must be laws to regulate, and especially there must be an adequate force of inspectors to enforce the laws.

5. There must be state inspection of important articles, on the safety or genuineness of which the public is not competent to pass, e.g., the safety of boilers or steamboats, the quality of milk, water or lighting gas, etc. On the other hand all questions of mere taste or convenience should be left to individuals.

6. Self-help is ineffective against corporations holding natural monopolies. The individual cannot cheapen car fares by refusing to ride, nor compel purer or cheaper gas by burning kerosene. The state by its franchise creates such monopolies; it is a partner in them; and it is responsible for their behavior.

7. But experience has shown that constant state interference is irksome to the corporations, corrupting to the state, and not always satisfactory to the public. Where state interference yields no remedy, state ownership should be fearlessly tried. The success of modern experiments in it amply justifies the trial. It is true that there are great potential dangers in it; but it is also true that there are great actual dangers and evils in our present system of farming out franchises.

Public ownership may build up a great bureaucracy; but our present system has actually built up in the great corporations a huge administrative organization, which is less amenable to public interest and public opinion than state officials. A great body of officeholders may indeed become a menace to free institutions; but our great corporations, dependent on legislatures and officials for privileges, are actually now the chief source of corruption in our public life. It is true that state ownership would do away with competition, check private initiative, and eliminate the element of personal ownership and management. But all that is being done now. Competition between railroads or gas companies is difficult to begin and more difficult to maintain. The minor stockholders of a railway have next to no voice in the management.

If it is our industrial destiny to submit to industrial centralization and its evils anyway, let us at least have the profits of centralization too, and the sense of ownership which public proprietorship would awaken in the people. If the state has often done its work badly, perhaps the remedy is not to withhold further work from it, but to make its work so large and so important to public comfort, that its performance will be jealously watched, and a higher standard of efficiency and fidelity will be set for our public servants. I believe it is fair to say that the experience of the past points away from state interference with natural monopolies and toward state ownership of them.

In conclusion, I would offer three suggestions to those who are afraid of socialism, dissatisfied with paternalism, and desirous to retain the largest possible measure of industrial individualism:

1. See that any lingering inequalities in our laws are purged out, so that if the workingman is to fight for himself, he will, at least, not have to fight with one hand strapped to his back. Brentano says: All statues of laborers in the Middle Ages were framed with regard to the powers and wants of the landed proprietors. Our legislation has come to us in unbroken continuity from a past when the lower classes did not help to make the laws. It is on the face of it unlikely that the short span of time during which the common people have had a voice in legislation, has sufficed to secure real equality in principle and practice. But until there is equality of law, self-help is unfair.

2. Help self-help. Help co-operative stores and profit-sharing along. Offer your services for the peaceful settlement of labor disputes. Extend the organization of labor. Back up just strikes. These are the means offered by self-help. If you trust in this Caesar, strengthen Caesar's hands.

3. Strengthen public opinion in its demands for justice and humanity. That is the silent arbiter in all our struggles for the right, the compulsory power in all progress. As long as the walking delegate is sneered at and labor leaders vilified by the religious and secular press; as long as good men concede it as self-evident that employers can do as they will with their own, and that "there is nothing to arbitrate," unless they please, so long self-help is helplessness. Remember that every great strike that fails, strengthens the impression that self-help is futile, and that salvation comes only by state help or socialism. If you wish to stave off socialism, stiffen the public opinion which backs up the labor movement. And that, gentlemen, is not done by silence.

*

ON MONOPOLIES

AT THE Baptist Congress for the discussion of current questions in Toronto, November 12, 1889, the following was contributed as part of the consideration of the topic above:

For the last three years I have been working in New York City, and by reason of the pity and sympathy which the Lord Jesus Christ has implanted in my heart, I have not been able to look on the things I see about me there unmoved, or without thinking on the causes of those sad appearances. I have done some reading and some thinking upon the matter, but very little speaking. I am glad to say, for the information of the gentlemen who questioned the accuracy of the preceding speaker's statement of the principles laid down by Henry George, that I have read Mr. George's book, that I revere and honor him as my teacher to some extent in these things.

I would like to take issue, from the very beginning, with some of the preliminary statements of the last speaker, who claimed that it is the purpose of Christianity to change the individual character of man, and then to leave it to that individual character to work out gradually the transformation of society. It is certainly true that it is one of the main objects of Christianity to change the individual life, and to implant in the heart of man the truth and love of the Lord Jesus Christ. But I claim that that is only one-half of the object of Christianity, that the other half is to bring in the Kingdom of God, and that the efforts of the Christian Church ought to be directed in a like measure to the accomplishment of that last object, and that not only indirectly, by changing the individual and gradually having the influence emanate from him, but directly, and then having the influence of society react upon the individual. I will use a few illustrations to make clear my meaning. There was a time when slavery was established in this country. There were at that time many Christian men living in the South whose hearts beat warm for Jesus Christ; yet very few found it in their hearts, or thought they saw the way clear, to free their slaves, to take upon themselves the immense loss which that entailed. But when society stepped in and emancipated the slave, public opinion immediately began to veer around, and there are now a very few men in the South who desire to bring about the old condition of things. There, you see that not only did individual character work upon society, but society worked upon the individual character. Not only does individual opinion, in regard to anything, gradually bring about a transformation of society, but when society is transformed, individual opinion is very rapidly transformed also.

To take another example. We know what a long and costly struggle it has been to achieve the independence of the people in the history of mankind; how every step has been wrestled for and wrung out of the hands of royalty and aristocracy. It has been so in our own country and Great Britian, and all over Europe. But since the great doctrine of personal liberty has once been affirmed in the French Revolution, there is no longer any question in regard to it among civilized men. Even the Czar of Russia in making his proclamations puts himself, ostensibly at least, on the ground that he is acting for the welfare of his people, that he is the chief servant of the state, not that the people exist for him, but that he exists for the people. That great theorem is now an axiom; it has been granted; it can no longer be denied; and that which was formerly the doctrine of the few only, is now fast becoming the doctrine of all. Therefore, I hold that it is the duty of all Christian men, and of the Christian Church also, to work in the first place toward the amelioration of personal character, and to have the influence from that emanate into society. Certainly, that is true.

But we must not be blind to the other half of the truth. We must also attack the wrongs of human society and the unjust laws of the community, to bring about righteousness through the Kingdom of God in the world, and then we shall also have an influence radiating from society and centering upon the individual. Starting with these assertions I now turn to the subject we have in hand.

The chief school of political economy is the school of freedom, holding the doctrine of *laissez faire*, in the higher sense of that word. It holds that if natural forces are allowed their free play, the individual will be able to develop his full individuality, and society will be made comparatively happy—as happy as it is possible to be here below. That is an old assumption—a most noble idea—and it has worked out many beneficent changes. But I assert that *laissez faire*, this complete freedom of the natural and social forces, does not exist in society as it is at present constituted. Men are not free today to do that which they would do. They are compelled and hindered on all sides. We cannot buy our goods from wherever we want to. If I send for books I should like to read from Germany, I have to pay a fine for doing so. I am not free to get my information where I please. I am not free to buy clothes in Toronto and take them back to New York. I should be punished by a custom-house officer on the way back. Nor are we free to utilize the natural forces about us freely and fully.

In New York City the thing which is, perhaps, the most valuable and the most desired of all things, is land, the place to stand on, to breathe on, the place to be happy in. But the natural forces which would reduce or raise the price of land, the price which I would have to pay for standing on any piece of ground, is not left free to the natural forces to determine. In the upper part of New York City, as all those who are conversant with the condition of the city know, there are vast tracts of land which would give beautiful houses to many of those who are crowded into the lower part of the city, which are absolutely held and cannot be got at any price, because those who hold them are able to hold them, and intend to hold them until they are still more valuable than they are today. That monopoly, that keeping out of play the natural forces, influences the price of land, and thereby influences the health and happiness and right to live, of human society.

I use this simply as an example, to point out to you that in our present condition of society we have not the full, fair, free play of the natural forces of economic or social life. They are being interfered with on all hands. We are speaking of monopolies this evening. A complete monopoly is only the highest development of something which exists from the very basis of society up. It is the capstone of the pyramid that lies below. That same tendency exists everywhere. For instance, even in England there is not a complete monopoly of land; that would mean that all the land would be in a single hand. It has not come to that yet. Still, the land is to a very large extent monopolized, because it is in the hands of a comparatively few people, and that influences the price of the land.

I say, when we are speaking of monopolies, we are speaking really of a wider social and economic phenomonon, of every interference with freedom—with the freedom of natural forces. These interferences are of two kinds; the first is the artificial, which is created by law. For instance, take one subject which is very fresh in all your minds, as I can tell from your reception of some of my remarks—the tariff creates an artificial monopoly. Suppose, for instance, there was only a single saltpeter mine in this Dominion of Canada. Suppose there were others in the United States, but that a tariff would be constructed to keep the saltpeter of the United States over there. That would really create a monopoly for the man who owned the saltpeter mine in Canada; and that monopoly would be an artificial monopoly, for, if that law had not been passed, the saltpeter from the United States could be brought over here, and that man could not raise the price of his saltpeter as high as he pleased;

he would have to come down to that price of the people in the States, for which they would be willing to bring it over here. Now, such an artificial monopoly can be repealed or done away with by repealing the law which created it, and I think I shall appeal to the sense of justice in all your hearts when I say that any monopolies which are artificial are not right. Any person who is in the enjoyment of benefits which inure to him alone, and which are given to him by the sufferings of others, has rights which he ought not to have. Therefore, I say it seems to me to be a very fundamental and simple proposition of equity that artificial monopolies ought not to exist, and any law that has created them ought to be abrogated and repealed.

Now, in regard to natural monopolies, so called. There are some things, as explained to you by the previous speaker, which can be done only by one party. Suppose, for instance, that a streetcar track were to be run through Jarvis street [Toronto] here. It would be impossible for two companies to compete in that, because there is only so much width of street, and if a double streetcar track is laid along there, that is all you want on that street. Therefore, if the public grants the right of laying tracks on that street to any one party that party has a complete monopoly of the privilege of running streetcars on it, has it not? Therefore that is a monopoly, and it is a natural monopoly, because it is in the nature of it a monopoly. Such monopolies have been granted very extensively. The city grants to private companies the right to lay water and gas mains. That, too, is a monopoly, because, naturally, the city will object to having its streets torn up by a number of rival companies, having a large number of mains laid parallel to each other.

Now, it is the state that grants that right to the railway company, because, unless the state grants the right to buy the land continuously, to condemn the property and buy it at a certain valuation, the company could never build that road. It has to be granted by the power of the whole community, and therefore that privilege really belongs to the community which grants it. It is granted by the community to the company in return for certain undertakings on the part of the company. Now, I question whether it is wise on the part of the community any longer to give away its natural monopolies. I question whether it is right any longer for the City of Toronto to give away its rights of way through its public streets, or for the state to give away its right of way for railways, because in some cases these monopolies break down, and in others they get very rich, either of which is undesirable for the community. If the state itself should undertake the construction of these things it would alike bear the loss and the profit, and the whole thing would tend in a wonderful way to the development of the whole country.

I have no time now to enter into this idea, but I would lay it down as my personal position that not only should artificial monopolies be abrogated by the repeal of the law which created them, but also that natural monopolies ought to be held and managed by that power to which they really belong, namely, the community. Mr. George has taught this proposition in his book. He is often called a Socialist, but it is very incorrect to call him so; he is not a Socialist, but the strongest opponent of socialism in the United States. He is a strong advocate of *laissez faire* in the highest sense of that term. Therefore he insists that artificial monopolies, such as the tariff, should be swept away, and that freedom should be given to the natural forces of society, and that natural monopolies should be owned and managed by the community to which they naturally belong. These are his propositions in regard to monopoly. Am I right?

Now, granting that that would be a good thing—that artificial monopoly should be done away with and natural monopolies held by the state—the question still remains whether there are not other lines of business which would still be monopolized, for instance, the manufacture of starch, the catching of fish, the curing of salt, or anything at all. Is there not a natural tendency in human society toward the aggregation of forces, toward grasping natural forces, and uniting to crush out opposition? This afternoon, in a way very interesting to me, the point was made that there is a universal tendency to co-operation, to the uniting of forces, and that is the case because united forces are immensely stronger than scattered forces. I have noticed sometimes the working of a pile driver. A great block of iron is hoisted up, bit by bit, to the top of a great beam, and then finally it is let loose and slides down with a tremendous impetus on the pile below and drives it into the earth. Now, imagine that great mass of iron broken up into small hammers, each weighing half a pound; imagine that these were placed in the hands of a great number of men, each one wanting to get the first chance to pound on the pile and drive it in. Do you think they would get it in as fast as by having the force repose in that great pile driver, which comes down with one great blow at once? It is the same with all things and all affairs; there is so much more strength in co-operation than in individual work. Therefore it seems to me very likely that even after free play has been secured for natural forces those who have already a large amount of force, or those who, by moral excellence or intellectual keenness, see the advantages of combination, will get together and after all have a monopoly.

There is where the socialists and Mr. George disagree. He says that after *laissez faire* has been secured, social ills would stop and go no further. The socialists say that even after that, we should still have many of the phenomena of social life that at present distress us, and I, for my part, cannot but think that they are right. Even after that, there would still be a power of the stronger over the weaker. Therefore I would put to you the question whether, besides natural and artificial monopolies, there is not also a necessary monopoly. Is it not, with the tendencies of our age, in the nature of the thing, inevitable that forces will finally be monopolized? If so, who has the right to hold that monopoly? Has any individual the right to hold it to the detriment of all? Has any combination of individuals the right to hold it to the detriment of all others? Or is that a privilege which belongs to all to hold? If a monopoly draws from all should not its benefits go to all? There is the whole thing in a nutshell. Mazzini, the great Italian martyr and liberator, points out that the French Revolution was not, as many have supposed, the beginning of a new era. He says it was merely the closing of the old era, and an affirmation on the civil and political side of life of what the Protestant Reformation affirmed on the religious side of life, viz., personal liberty. That has now been accepted; there is no doubt about that any more; it is only working its way slowly into human institutions, but it is there now in human thought; you can never take it away again. Now, he says, the new era is beginning. We have come now to the era of co-operation and association, and all these attempts at combining and associating which we see about us in every sphere of life are only humanity's blind gropings and its feeling through the dark toward the goal which Christ himself has pointed out to us.

*

THE INTERPENETRATION OF THE LIFE
OF CHURCH AND STATE

" RELATION of Church and State" was the theme of a session of the Baptist Congress for the discussion of current questions at Toronto, November 13, 1889. The following was given in the course of the discussion:

In the old times Count Eberhard, of Württemberg, had a feud with his own son Ulrich, and in order to demonstrate how thorough was their separation, he cut the tablecloth between them as they sat at meat together. I have seen this evening the cutting of the tablecloth—the complete separation announced. But it seems to me that only one side of the principle has been announced, for all the enunciations have been negative, and not very many of them positive. We have heard here the ultimate statement of the Baptist doctrine—complete separation of church and state. But I read a short time ago the life of that great and noble man. Thomas Arnold of Rugby, and also that of Frederick Dennison Maurice; and I remember that they held the view that the church and state are necessarily, and in their nature, one.

Here we have two views, that are at opposite poles from each other. Is either one of them absolutely false? Shall we say that this latter view is so wrong that we will have to condemn it to the uttermost depths of Tophet? Or shall we take the position that there is a way between the two? No, I don't say that. Let us not be of the men who are forever making compromises, and believing in the *via media*; let us assume the higher wisdom that says not that the one is true and the other untrue, but that both of them in some way are true. I hold that both of these views have the element of truth in them, but that either is incomplete without the other. Would you accept this formula, that there must be complete division in the *organizations* of religion and state, but that there must be an interpenetration of the *life* of church and state? Does that seem to you true? There must be a complete division of the organizations, because unless the church organization is completely divided from the state organization, the state organization will influence the church, and will hinder it from exercising its true functions; therefore we must divide the two absolutely and utterly. But on the other hand, the two must interpenetrate in their influences and in their life, somehow or other. The attempt has been made frequently enough to divorce the two.

In the French Revolution the effort was made not only to sever the connection between the institutions of the church and the institutions of the state, but to cast out religion itself, and we know that that was disastrous. We know also that attempts have been made to sever the connection between the life of the church and the life of the state; but I remember that God himself said some things to us about that; he said something to us about those who believe in a multitude of sacrifices, in the lifting up of hands in prayer, and in the solemn assemblies, but who turn not aside to lift up the fallen, to bring to justice those who oppress the widow and the fatherless, and to help the needy; and I remember that his condemnation on those who thus believed only in the church and kept their hands away from the state, was of the most severe kind.

The two must somehow interpenetrate. There is a positive side to this question, and not a negative side only. The state must be built on righteousness. Its very purpose is to exercise righteousness among men, and its ultimate goal is to be merged in the Kingdom of God which is to come on earth. The kingdoms of this world shall become the kingdoms of the Christ, and the day shall come when every knee shall bow and every tongue shall confess that Jesus Christ is Lord, to the glory of God the Father. That is the ultimate glorious ideal toward which the whole organization of the world must be tending. That is the ideal of the state. Now, what has the church to do with it? I believe in the prophetic ministry of the Christian church within the state. I believe that the church is composed of men who are touched with the power of the life to come, with the power of the *aion mellon*, of the world era that is coming. They see the things that shall be in the future, but which are not yet. The church must announce those things in the ears of the state; it must declare that truth which is not yet recognized; it must perform that duty which has not yet been performed; and if necessary, it must suffer in doing so, and in suffering and in declaring the truth, and in doing that which is right, it shall usher in the reign of righteousness throughout the kingdoms of the world. That is the positive connection which the church must necessarily have with the state.

Brethren, I feel sometimes that in our strong statements of the separation between church and state, we have come to gather up our skirts and to act as if the state had no more claim on us; that somehow our life as Christians and as citizens can be cut asunder; that on one side we can be Christians and on the other side we can be citizens. It is not true. We must be the two things at the same time, and we can be that in just one way—by being animated by the life of Jesus Christ, and by carrying that life into the state in every direction.

*

THE PULPIT IN RELATION TO POLITICAL
AND SOCIAL REFORM

*A*T THE 10th Annual Session of the Baptist Congress, for the discussion of current questions, May 19, 1892, in Philadelphia, the following comments were made in the course of discussion of the above theme. They were printed in full, pp. 127–29, of the Proceedings, New York, Baptist Congress Publishing Company, 1892. Dr. Rauschenbusch was corresponding secretary and treasurer of the Congress.

I want to lay before you a few plain, candid propositions:

My first proposition is that the whole aim of Christ is embraced in the words "the kingdom of God"; that this ideal is for this side of death, and not for the other side; that it is a social ideal and not an individualist idea; and that in that ideal is embraced the sanctification of all life, the regeneration of humanity, and the reformation of all social institutions.

Second, the church is the organ to accomplish this work. It is the body of Christ, through which his spirit works, and makes itself felt on earth. Therefore every department of human life which has not been sanctified and brought under the obedience of Jesus Christ is a province to be reclaimed for him by the church.

Third, the fundamental work of the church is in the dissemination of ideas, and the spread of convictions. Therefore if there are false convictions concerning any relation of human life, the first thing for the church to do is to spread the right convictions. And that is done by preaching. We shall have to make men see things as Jesus Christ saw them, or as he would see them if he were walking among us today. Therefore we shall have to treat social and political questions just so far as there are righteousness and love in them. If it is a question of utility, it does not concern the church. If it is a question whether a streetcar company ought to use electricity or cable power, the church has nothing to do with that; that is a question for civil engineers. But if it is a question whether the streetcar companies are to own Philadelphia, or Philadelphia is to own the streetcars, that is a question of righteousness.

Fourth, the best time to preach on political questions, is before they have become political questions; before they have been thrown out into the general wrangle and snarl of politics; before they have become partisan matters. After they have become so, it is impossible not to become a partisan in discussing them. The Christian church has the duty of treating questions, before the world treats them. Jesus said: "If your righteousness exceed not the righteousness of the Scribes and Pharisees, you are not fit for the kingdom of God." In the same way, I say, unless you see righteousness before the world sees it, you are not fit for the kingdom of God.

Fifth, cases may arise where questions of righteousness and love have become political issues, the predominating political issues, and when things are so balanced, that the church will have to throw its weight on the one side or the other, if righteousness is to be done. In such cases as the lottery conflict in Louisiana, it is the duty of the church to spring forward and to throw itself into the conflict. At such times, prudent conservatism is more unChristlike and far more dangerous than the most headlong impetuosity.

Sixth, when individuals, as will occasionally be the case, feel the call upon them by some personal adaption or by some need arising in their life, of throwing themselves completely into political or social agitation, men of the church, ministers, laymen, the church should back them up as much as possible. Such has been the case with Stoecker in Germany, Dr. Parkhurst in New York, and others we could think of. If such a man feels it his duty to go forward and leave church work proper, the church should pray for him while he is wading in the swamp for others.

Seventh, if the church should leave political and social questions aside, and address itself only to individual and family morality, men will nevertheless be interested in politics. If they are men they will. And if you give them in the church only the morality and ideal of the individual and family, and leave the ideal of society at large and of the state to be treated in the press and elsewhere, there will be a severing of the unity of life. Such a dividing of life is fatal to the rounded ideal of Christian holiness and consecration.

Eighth, if we should leave these issues to be treated by others, we should infallibly lose the people. They have been lost on the continent of Europe. The church there, like Esau, is trying to regain the birthright it has lost. It now goes to the workingmen and says: "The church is your friend. We are anxious to do all these things for you workingmen." But the church brought its desolation on its own head. My brethren, let not the church in America fail in this, its hour of trial. The hour is coming for us, and the question will be whether we gloriously lead or ignominiously follow.

Ninth, in case we should leave these things behind, it would bring disease into the life of the church, instead of saving the life of the church for spiritual work. It would actually rot the church. It is now doing so.

And finally, tenth, the last caution is this: If we treat political and social questions, let us not treat them from the standpoint of ecclesiastical politics. That is the reason, and the good reason, why the cry has gone out: "Let the priests and parsons keep out of politics." They have too often entered politics for the aggrandizement of the church, not for the aggrandizement of the nation. Let the church be faithful and say to the people: "We want nothing for ourselves; we are ready to give all for you." Then we may safely assume a position of leadership in embodying the law of Christ in the laws of our country.

The Little Gate to God

In the castle of my soul
Is a little garden gate,
Whereat, when I enter
I am in the presence of God.
In a moment, in the turning of a thought,
I am where God is,
This is a fact. . . .

When I enter into God,
All life has a meaning,
Without asking I know;
My desires are even now fulfilled,
My fever is gone,
In the great quiet of God.
My troubles are but pebbles on the road,
My joys are like the everlasting hills. . . .

So it is when my soul steps through the postern gate
Into the presence of God.
Big things become small, and small things become great.
The near becomes far, and the future is near,
The lowly and despised is shot through with glory. . . .
God is the substance of all resolutions;
When I am in him, I am in the Kingdom of God
And in the Fatherland of my Soul.

[1918]

An Affirmation of Faith

I AFFIRM my faith in the reality of the spiritual world, in the sacred voice of duty, in the compelling power of truth and holiness, in prayer, in the life eternal, in Him who is the life of my life and the reality behind all things visible. I rejoice to believe in God.

I affirm my faith in the Kingdom of God and my hope in its final triumph. I determine by faith to live day by day within the higher order and the divine peace of my true fatherland, and to carry its spirit and laws into all my dealings in the world that now is.

I make an act of love toward all fellow men. I accept them as they are, with all their sins and failures, and declare my solidarity with them. If any have wronged or grieved me, I place my mind with the all-comprehending and all-loving mind of God, and here and now forgive. I desire to minister God's love to men and to offer no hindrance to the free flow of his love through me.

I affirm my faith in life. I call life good and not evil. I accept the limitations of my own life and believe it is possible for me to live a beautiful and Christlike life within the conditions set for me. Through the power of Christ which descends on me, I know that I can be more than conqueror.

[1918]

* XI *

Prayers of the Social Awakening

*N*OTES on Rauschenbusch's prayers have been given above, preceding his statement, "The Social Meaning of the Lord's Prayer." This selection of readings must include the full texts of a number of the prayers. They illustrate Rauschenbusch's persistent interest in the personal prayer life. They came from the crowded ways of life; they arose out of sympathy with people in need; they were concerned with others rather than with the author of the petitions. If there are any who think that Rauschenbusch ever neglected personal religion for the social gospel, it may be noted that he believed that "in the best social order that is conceivable, men will still smoulder with lust and ambition and be lashed by hate and jealousy, as with the whip of a slave driver." (Christianizing the Social Order, p. 104.)

The following prayers are selected from a much larger number that were published in 1910 and 1925 by the Pilgrim Press, Boston:

*

FOR THE FATHERHOOD OF GOD

O THOU great Father of us all, we rejoice that at last we know thee. All our soul within us is glad because we need no longer cringe before thee as slaves of holy fear, seeking to appease thine anger by sacrifice and self-inflicted pain, but may come like little children, trustful and happy, to the God of love. Thou art the only true father, and all the tender beauty of our human loves is the reflected radiance of thy loving kindness, like the moonlight from the sunlight, and testifies to the eternal passion that kindled it.

Grant us growth of spiritual vision, that with the passing years we may enter into the fullness of this our faith. Since thou art our Father, may we not hide our sins from thee, but overcome them by the stern comfort of thy presence. By this knowledge uphold us in our sorrows

150

and make us patient even amid the unsolved mysteries of the years. Reveal to us the larger goodness and love that speak through the unbending laws of thy world. Through this faith make us the willing equals of all thy other children.

As thou art ever pouring out thy life in sacrificial father-love, may we accept the eternal law of the cross and give ourselves to thee and to all men. We praise thee for Jesus Christ, whose life has revealed to us this faith and law, and we rejoice that he has become the first-born among many brethren. Grant that in us, too, the faith in thy fatherhood may shine through all our life with such persuasive beauty that some who still creep in the dusk of fear may stand erect as free sons of God, and that others who now through unbelief are living as orphans in an empty world may stretch out their hands to the great Father of their spirits and find thee near.

*

FOR THIS WORLD

O GOD, we thank thee for this universe, our great home; for its vastness and its riches, and for the manifoldness of the life which teems upon it and of which we are part. We praise thee for the arching sky and the blessed winds, for the driving clouds and the constellations on high. We praise thee for the salt sea and the running water, for the everlasting hills, for the trees, and for the grass under our feet. We thank thee for our senses by which we can see the splendor of the morning, and hear the jubilant songs of love, and smell the breath of the springtime. Grant us, we pray thee, a heart wide open to all this joy and beauty, and save our souls from being so steeped in care or so darkened by passion that we pass heedless and unseeing when even the thornbush by the wayside is aflame with the glory of God.

Enlarge within us the sense of fellowship with all the living things, our little brothers, to whom thou hast given this earth as their home in common with us. We remember with shame that in the past we have exercised the high dominion of man with ruthless cruelty, so that the voice of the Earth, which should have gone up to thee in song, has been a groan of travail. May we realize that they live, not for us alone, but for themselves and for thee, and that they love the sweetness of life even as we, and serve thee in their place better than we in ours.

When our use of this world is over and we make room for others, may we not leave anything ravished by our greed or spoiled by our ignorance, but may we hand on our common heritage fairer and sweeter through our use of it, undiminished in fertility and joy, that so our bodies may return in peace to the great mother who nourished them and our spirits may round the circle of a perfect life in thee.

*

FOR CHILDREN WHO WORK

O THOU great Father of the weak, lay thy hand tenderly on all the little children on earth and bless them. Bless our own children, who are life of our life, and who have become the heart of our heart. Bless every little child-friend that has leaned against our knee and refreshed our soul by its smiling trustfulness. Be good to all children who long in vain for human love, or for flowers and water, and the sweet breast of Nature. But bless with a sevenfold blessing the young lives whose slender shoulders are already bowed beneath the yoke of toil, and whose glad growth is being stunted forever. Suffer not their little bodies to be utterly sapped, and their minds to be given over to stupidity and the vices of an empty soul. We have all jointly deserved the millstone of thy wrath for making these little ones to stumble and fall. Grant all employers of labor stout hearts to refuse enrichment at such a price. Grant to all the citizens and officers of states which now permit this wrong the grace of holy anger. Help us to realize that every child of our nation is in very truth our child, a member of our great family. By the Holy Child that nestled in Mary's bosom; by the memories of our own childhood joys and sorrows; by the sacred possibilities that slumber in every child, we beseech thee to save us from killing the sweetness of young life by the greed of gain.

*

FOR WOMEN WHO TOIL

O GOD, we pray thee for our sisters who are leaving the ancient shelter of the home to earn their wage in the factory and the store amid the press of modern life. Save them from the strain of unremitting toil that would unfit them for the holy duties of home and motherhood which the future may lay upon them. Give them grace to cherish under the new surroundings the old sweetness and gentleness of womanhood, and in the rough mingling of life to keep their hearts pure and their lives untarnished. Save them from the terrors of utter want. Teach them to stand loyally by their sisters, that by united action they may better their common lot.

If it must be so that our women toil like men, help us still to reverence in them the mothers of the future. But make us determined to shield them from unequal burdens, that the women of our nation be not drained of strength and hope for the enrichment of a few, lest our homes grow poor in the wifely sweetness and motherly love which have been the saving strength and glory of our country. To such as yearn for the love and sovereign freedom of their own home, grant in due time the fulfillment of their sweet desires. By Mary, the beloved, who bore the world's redemption in her bosom; by the memory of our own dear mothers who kissed our souls awake; by the little daughters who must soon go out into that world which we are now fashioning for others, we beseech thee that we may deal aright by all women.

*

FOR EMPLOYERS

WE INVOKE thy grace and wisdom, O Lord, upon all men of good will who employ and control the labor of men. Amid the numberless irritations and anxieties of their position, help them to keep a quiet and patient temper, and to rule firmly and wisely, without harshness and anger. Since they hold power over the bread, the safety, and the hopes of the workers, may they wield their powers justly and with love, as older brothers and leaders in the great fellowship of labor. Suffer not the heavenly light of compassion for the weak and the old to be quenched in their hearts. When they are tempted to follow the ruthless ways of others, and to sacrifice human health and life for profit, do thou strengthen their will in the hour of need, and bring to naught the counsels of the heartless. Save them from repressing their workers into sullen submission and helpless fear. May they not sin against the Christ by using the bodies and souls of men as mere tools to make things, forgetting the human hearts and longings of these their brothers.

Raise up among us employers who shall be makers of men as well as of goods. Give us masters of industry who will use their higher ability and knowledge in lifting the workers to increasing independence and vigor, and who will train their helpers for the larger responsibilities of the coming age. Give us men of faith who will see beyond the strife of the present and catch a vision of a nobler organization of our work, when all will still follow the leadership of the ablest, not in fear but by the glad will of all, and when none shall be master and none shall be man, but all shall stand side by side in a strong and righteous brotherhood of work.

*

FOR WRITERS AND NEWSPAPERMEN

O THOU great source of truth and knowledge, we remember before thee all whose calling it is to gather and winnow the facts for informing the people. Inspire them with a determined love for honest work and a stanch hatred for the making of lies, lest the judgments of our nation be perverted and we be taught to call light darkness and darkness light. Since the sanity and wisdom of a nation are in their charge, may they count in shame to set the baser passions of men on fire for the sake of gain. May they never suffer themselves to be used in drugging the mind of the people with falsehood and prejudice.

Grant them boldness to turn the unwelcome light on those who love the darkness because their deeds are evil. Put into their hands the shining sword of truth, and make them worthy successors of the great champions of the people who held truth to be a holy thing by which nations live and for which men should die. Cause them to realize that they have a public function in the commonwealth, and that their country may be saved by their courage or undone by their cowardice and silence. Grant them the heart of manhood to cast their mighty influence with the forces that make the people strong and free, and if they suffer loss, may they rejoice in that as proof to their own souls that they have fought a good fight and have been servants of the higher law.

*

FOR MINISTERS

O JESUS, we thy ministers bow before thee to confess the common sins of our calling. Thou knowest all things; thou knowest that we love thee and that our hearts' desire is to serve thee in faithfulness; and yet, like Peter, we have so often failed thee in the hour of thy need. If ever we have loved our own leadership and power when we sought to lead our people to thee, we pray thee to forgive. If we have been engrossed in narrow duties and little questions, when the vast needs of humanity called aloud for prophetic vision and apostolic sympathy, we pray thee to forgive. If in our loyalty to the church of the past we have distrusted thy living voice and have suffered thee to pass from our door unheard, we pray thee to forgive. If ever we have been more concerned for the strong and the rich than for the shepherdless throngs of the people for whom thy soul grieved, we pray thee to forgive.

O Master, amidst our failures we cast ourselves upon thee in humility and contrition. We need new light and a new message. We need the ancient spirit of prophecy and the leaping fire and joy of a new conviction, and thou alone canst give it. Inspire the ministry of thy church with dauntless courage to face the vast needs of the future. Free us from all entanglements that have hushed our voice and bound our action. Grant us grace to look upon the veiled sins of the rich and the coarse vices of the poor through thine eyes. Give us thine inflexible sternness against sin, and thine inexhaustible compassion for the frailty and tragedy of those who do the sin. Make us faithful shepherds of thy flock, true seers of God, and true followers of Jesus.

*

FOR THE BABIES [1]

Written for the Milk and Baby Hygiene Association of Boston

O GOD, since thou hast laid the little children into our arms in utter helplessness, with no protection save our love, we pray that the sweet appeal of their baby hands may not be in vain. Let no innocent life in our city be quenched again in useless pain through our ignorance and sin. May we who are mothers or fathers seek eagerly to join wisdom to our love, lest love itself be deadly when unguided by knowledge. Bless the doctors and nurses, and all the friends of men, who are giving of their skill and devotion to the care of our children. If there are any who were kissed by love in their own infancy, but who have no child to whom they may give as they have received, grant them such largeness of sympathy that they may rejoice to pay their debt in full to all children who have need of them.

Forgive us, our Father, for the heartlessness of the past. Grant us great tenderness for all babes who suffer, and a growing sense of the divine mystery that is brooding in the soul of every child.

[1] First published by The Survey.

*

MORITURI TE SALUTANT

O THOU Eternal One, we who are doomed to die lift up our souls to thee for strength, for Death has passed us in the throng of men and touched us, and we know that at some turn of our pathway he stands waiting to take us by the hand and lead us—we know not whither. We praise thee that to us he is no more an enemy but thy great angel and our friend, who alone can open for some of us the prison house of pain and misery and set our feet in the roomy spaces of a larger life. Yet we are but children, afraid of the dark and the unknown, and we dread the parting from the life that is so sweet and from the loved ones who are so dear.

Grant us of thy mercy a valiant heart, that we may tread the road with head uplifted and a smiling face. May we do our work to the last with a wholesome joy, and love our loves with an added tenderness because the days of love are short. On thee we cast the heaviest burden that numbs our soul, the gnawing fear for those we love, whom we must leave unsheltered in a selfish world. We trust in thee, for through all our years thou hast been our stay. O thou Father of the fatherless, put thy arm about our little ones! And ere we go, we pray that the days may come when the dying may die unafraid, because men have ceased to prey on the weak, and the great family of the nation enfolds all with its strength and care.

We thank thee that we have tasted the rich life of humanity. We bless thee for every hour of life, for all our share in the joys and strivings of our brothers, for the wisdom gained which will be part of us forever. If soon we must go, yet through thee we have lived and our life flows on in the race. By thy grace we too have helped to shape the future and bring in the better day.

If our spirit droops in loneliness, uphold us by thy companionship. When all the voices of love grow faint and drift away, thy everlasting arms will still be there. Thou art the Father of our spirits; from thee we have come; to thee we go. We rejoice that in the hours of our purer vision, when the pulse throb of thine eternity is strong within us, we know that no pang of mortality can reach our unconquerable soul, and that for those who abide in thee death is but the gateway to life eternal. Into thy hands we commend our spirit.

*

A PRAYER OF WRATH: AGAINST WAR

O LORD, since first the blood of Abel cried to thee from the ground that drank it, this earth of thine has been defiled with the blood of man shed by his brother's hand, and the centuries sob with the ceaseless horror of war. Ever the pride of kings and the covetousness of the strong have driven peaceful nations to slaughter. Ever the songs of the past and the pomp of armies have been used to inflame the passions of the people. Our spirit cries out to thee in revolt against it, and we know that our righteous anger is answered by thy holy wrath.

Break thou the spell of the enchantments that make the nations drunk with the lust of battle and draw them on as willing tools of death. Grant us a quiet and steadfast mind when our own nation clamors for vengeance or aggression. Strengthen our sense of justice and our regard for the equal worth of other peoples and races. Grant to the rulers of nations faith in the possibility of peace through justice, and grant to the common people a new and stern enthusiasm for the cause of peace. Bless our soldiers and sailors for their swift obedience and their willingness to answer to the call of duty, but inspire them none the less with a hatred of war, and may they never for love of private glory or advancement provoke its coming. May our young men still rejoice to die for their country with the valor of their fathers, but teach our age nobler methods of matching our strength and more effective ways of giving our life for the flag.

O thou strong Father of all nations, draw all thy great family together with an increasing sense of our common blood and destiny, that peace may come on earth at last, and thy sun may shed its light rejoicing on a holy brotherhood of peoples.

*

FOR THE KINGDOM OF GOD

O CHRIST, thou hast bidden us pray for the coming of thy Father's Kingdom, in which his righteous will shall be done on earth. We have treasured thy words, but we have forgotten their meaning, and thy great hope has grown dim in thy church. We bless thee for the inspired souls of all ages who saw afar the shining city of God, and by faith left the profit of the present to follow their vision. We rejoice that today the hope of these lonely hearts is becoming the clear faith of millions. Help us, O Lord, in the courage of faith to seize what has now come so near, that the glad day of God may dawn at last. As we have mastered Nature that we might gain wealth, help us now to master the social relations of mankind that we may gain justice and a world of brothers. For what shall it profit our nation if it gain numbers and riches, and lose the sense of the living God and the joy of human brotherhood?

Make us determined to live by truth and not by lies, to found our common life on the eternal foundations of righteousness and love, and no longer to prop the tottering house of wrong by legalized cruelty and force. Help us to make the welfare of all the supreme law of our land, that so our commonwealth may be built strong and secure on the love of all its citizens. Cast down the throne of Mammon who ever grinds the life of men, and set up thy throne, O Christ, for thou didst die that men might live. Show thy erring children at last the way from the City of Destruction to the City of Love, and fulfill the longings of the Prophets of humanity. Our Master, once more we make thy faith our prayer: "Thy kingdom come! Thy will be done on earth!"

*

FOR THE PROPHETS AND PIONEERS

WE PRAISE thee, Almighty God, for thine elect, the prophets and martyrs of humanity, who gave their thoughts and prayers and agonies for the truth of God and the freedom of the people. We praise thee that amid loneliness and the contempt of men, in poverty and imprisonment, when they were condemned by the laws of the mighty and buffeted on the scaffold, thou didst uphold them by thy spirit in loyalty to thy holy cause.

Our hearts burn within us as we follow the bleeding feet of thy Christ down the centuries, and count the mounts of anguish on which he was crucified anew in his prophets and the true apostles of his spirit. Help us to forgive those who did it, for some truly thought they were serving thee when they suppressed thy light, but oh, save us from the same mistake! Grant us an unerring instinct for what is right and true, and a swift sympathy to divine those who truly love and serve the people. Suffer us not by thoughtless condemnation or selfish opposition to weaken the arm and chill the spirit of those who strive for the redemption of mankind. May we never bring upon us the blood of all the righteous by renewing the spirit of those who persecuted them in the past. Grant us rather that we, too, may be counted in the chosen band of those who have given their life as a ransom for the many. Send us forth with the pathfinders of humanity to lead thy people another day's march toward the land of promise.

And if we, too, must suffer loss, and drink of the bitter pool of misunderstanding and scorn, uphold us by thy Spirit in steadfastness and joy because we are found worthy to share in the work and the reward of Jesus and all the saints.

*

FOR OUR CITY

O GOD, we pray thee for this, the city of our love and pride. We rejoice in her spacious beauty and her busy ways of commerce, in her stores and factories where hand joins hand in toil, and in her blessed homes where heart joins heart for rest and love.

Help us to make our city the mighty common workshop of our people, where everyone will find his place and task, in daily achievement building up his own life to resolute manhood, keen to do his best with hand and mind. Help us to make our city the greater home of our people, where all may live their lives in comfort, unafraid, loving their loves in peace and rounding out their years in strength.

Bind our citizens, not by the bond of money and of profit alone, but by the glow of neighborly good will, by the thrill of common joys, and the pride of common possessions. As we set the greater aims for the future of our city, may we ever remember that her true wealth and greatness consist, not in the abundance of the things we possess, but in the justice of her institutions and the brotherhood of her children. Make her rich in her sons and daughters and famous through the lofty passions that inspire them.

We thank thee for the patriot men and women of the past whose generous devotion to the common good has been the making of our city. Grant that our own generation may build worthily on the foundation they have laid. If in the past there have been some who have sold the city's good for private gain, staining her honor by their cunning and greed, fill us, we beseech thee, with the righteous anger of true sons that we may purge out the shame lest it taint the future years.

Grant us a vision of our city, fair as she might be: a city of justice, where none shall prey on others; a city of plenty, where vice and poverty shall cease to fester; a city of brotherhood, where all success shall be founded on service, and honor shall be given to nobleness alone; a city of peace, where order shall not rest on force, but on the love of all for the city, the great mother of the common life and weal. Hear thou, O Lord, the silent prayer of all our hearts as we each pledge our time and strength and thought to speed the day of her coming beauty and righteousness.

*

FOR THE CO-OPERATIVE COMMONWEALTH

O GOD, we praise thee for the dream of the golden city of peace and righteousness which has ever haunted the prophets of humanity, and we rejoice with joy unspeakable that at last the people have conquered the freedom and knowledge and power which may avail to turn into reality the vision that so long has beckoned in vain.

Speed now the day when the plains and the hills and the wealth thereof shall be the people's own, and thy freemen shall not live as tenants of men on the earth which thou hast given to all; when no babe shall be born without its equal birthright in the riches and knowledge wrought out by the labor of the ages; and when the mighty engines of industry shall throb with a gladder music because the men who ply these great tools shall be their owners and masters.

Bring to an end, O Lord, the inhumanity of the present, in which all men are ridden by the pale fear of want while the nation of which they are citizens sits throned amid the wealth of their making; when the manhood in some is cowed by helplessness, while the soul of others is surfeited and sick with power which no frail son of the dust should wield.

O God, save us, for our nation is at strife with its own soul and is sinning against the light which thou aforetime hast kindled in it. Thou hast called our people to freedom, but we are withholding from men their share in the common heritage without which freedom becomes a hollow name. Thy Christ has kindled in us the passion for brotherhood, but the social life we have built, denies and slays brotherhood.

We pray thee to revive in us the hardy spirit of our forefathers that we may establish and complete their work, building on the basis of their democracy the firm edifice of a co-operative commonwealth, in which both government and industry shall be of the people, by the

people, and for the people. May we, who now live, see the oncoming
of the great day of God, when all men shall stand side by side in equal
worth and real freedom, all toiling and all reaping, masters of nature
but brothers of men, exultant in the tide of the common life, and
jubilant in the adoration of thee, the source of their blessings and the
Father of all.

*

THE AUTHOR'S PRAYER

O THOU who art the light of my soul, I thank thee for the incomparable joy of listening to thy voice within, and I know that no
word of thine shall return void, however brokenly uttered. If aught in
this book was said through lack of knowledge, or through weakness of
faith in thee or of love for men, I pray thee to overrule my sin and turn
aside its force before it harm thy cause. Pardon the frailty of thy servant, and look upon him only as he sinks his life in Jesus, his Master
and Saviour.

* XII *

A Letter to One Entering the Ministry

WALTER RAUSCHENBUSCH

DEPARTMENT OF CHURCH HISTORY
Rochester Theological Seminary
Rochester, N. Y.

May 18th, 1911.

Dear Sir:—

Through the generosity of a friend I am enabled to present this copy of "Christianity and the Social Crisis" to you as a gift on your entrance into the Christian ministry. It is his hope that it will be a leaven in your life and work.

The ministry is the greatest and most glorious of all professions. Yet actually it has often narrowed the men who have entered it. It is of the highest importance that you lay hold of your life's task—whether at home or abroad—in the spirit of a missionary, as an apostle of a mighty Gospel that is to revolutionize both men and institutions, and to turn the anarchy and sinfulness of our present life into a kingdom of peace and love.

It is the hope of the giver and the writer that this book will help you to see and to face the larger tasks of Christianity, and we send you Good Cheer as you join the ranks of the greatest army that ever was.

Yours for the Kingdom of God,
(Signed) Walter Rauschenbusch.

Walter Rauschenbusch: A Chronology

Born, October 4, 1861, at Rochester, N. Y.

Childhood years in Germany, 1865–69.

Attended private school and free academy in Rochester, N. Y., 1869–79.

Spent summers on a farm in Lycoming County, Pa., 1870–79.

Baptized on confession of his faith, Rochester, N. Y., 1879.

Studied in Germany, 1879–83.

Studied at the University of Rochester and Rochester Theological Seminary, Rochester, N. Y., 1883–86.

Appointed as "summer supply" in a small Baptist church in Louisville, Ky., 1884.

Minister of the Second German Baptist Church, in Hell's Kitchen, New York, N. Y., 1886–97.

Supported Henry George in his campaign for mayor of New York, 1886.

Editor of *For the Right*, a Christian Socialist periodical, New York, 1889–91.

One of the initiators of the Brotherhood of the Kingdom, 1892.

Married Pauline Rather, a teacher in the public schools of Milwaukee, Wis., 1893.

Appointed to the German Department of Rochester Theological Seminary, 1897; to the chair of church history, Rochester Theological Seminary (now the Colgate-Rochester Divinity School), 1902.

Died, July 25, 1918, at Rochester, N. Y.

Index

Abbott, Lyman, 31, 89
Action, social, proposed, 22–29
Addams, Jane, 39
Affirmation of faith, 149
Altgeld, John Peter, 128
Apostolate of Christianity, 24–25, 27
Arnold, Thomas, 144

Baker, Ray Stannard, 77
Baptist Church, Second German, New York, 2
Baptist Congress for discussion of social current questions, 128–47
Brotherhood of the Kingdom, xvii
Brown, William Adams, 115
Bryan, William Jennings, viii, 38, 128

Calvinism, 59
Carnegie, Andrew, 76
Challenge to theology, 104
Christian Church, origins of, 94–95
Christian idea of God, 119–27, 150–51
  (See also Kingdom of God)
Christian influence on social order, 66–70
Christian institutions, as handicaps to Christianity, 16–18
Christian socialism, xx, 38
Christianity, and social crisis, 1–29
  Fraternal helpfulness of, 15
  Industrial revolution and, 18–19
  Love and, 86–88
  Primitive expressions of, 14–16
  Relation to social reconstruction, 16–18
Christians and Christianity, 99
Christians, social mission of, 90–91
Churches and socialism, 55–61
Churches, as fully Christian, 66
Church, and social crisis, 1–29
  Primitive institutions, 14–16
  Social movements and church, 20–22

Church-state relations, 143–45
College men and women, courses for, 89–101
Communism in primitive societies, 23
  Rauschenbusch on, xx
Conception of God, 119–27
Conversion of the strong, 62–72
Co-operatives, 21, 48–49, 81–82, 137
Corporate nature of evil, 109–11
Corporations, modern, 48–49, 51, 138–43
Crisis, caused by industrial revolution, 18–19

Democracy vs. autocracy, 107

Early Christianity, 14–16
Economic history, lessons of, 135
Eichhorn, Albert, 64
Ethical concepts of salvation, 133–35
Ely, Richard T., xvii, 59

Faith for social tasks, 42–47
Fatherhood of God, 150–51
Federal Council of Churches, 31, 73
Ford, Henry, 30, 76
Fosdick, Harry Emerson, vii, xiii–xxii, 2
Fraternal helpfulness, 15
  Organizations in society, 23
French revolution, 144

Gate to God, Little, 148
Gary, Elbert H., 1
George, Henry, xvii, 52–54, 142
Gladden, Washington, xvii
God, conception of, 119–27
  Fatherhood of, 150–51
  Social product, 120
  (See also Kingdom of God)
Gough, John B., 69
Greatest movement in history, 94

Hebrew prophets' teachings, 5–10
Hoover, Herbert, 102

Individualism of Christians, 18–22, 43–45, 66
Individualism of Church members, 18–22, 43–45, 66
Industrial revolution, effects of, 18–19

Jesus, teachings of Kingdom of God, xx, xxii, 3, 11–13, 20–22, 24, 28, 61, 72, 91, 99, 111–19
    Distinctive contribution of, 93
    Evolutionary consciousness of, 12, 43–44
    Initiator of Kingdom, 91, 99
    Master of life, 93
    Social aims of, 10–14
    Social ideals of, 95
    Social meaning of Lord's Prayer, 30–36
    Social principles of, 89–101
    Social reformer, 14
Joan of Arc, 65
Johnson, Tom, 1, 69
Judaism, 62

Kingdom of God, xx, xxii, 3, 11, 13, 20–22, 24, 28, 61–62, 72, 91, 99, 111–19, 149, 157
    Initiator of, 91, 99
    Theological significance of the concept, 111–19
    (See also Conception of God, Fatherhood of God)
Kingdom of Truth, 92

Labor movement, American, 2–3, 50–52
Labor Sunday, 73–74
Landis, Kenesaw Mountain, 1
Letter to one entering ministry, 162
Litany, social, 73–75
Lord's Prayer, social meaning of, 30–36
Love in society, 77–88
    Between man and woman, 78
    Paul's teachings on, 77, 84
    Rejuvenates life, 85
    Social progress and, 80
    Society-making force of, 81–83
Lowell, James Russell, 26
Luther, Martin, 13, 69

Marx, Karl, xx
    (See also Socialism)
Maurice, Frederick Denison, 144
McConnell, Francis J., 2
Mental transformation, through Christianity, 92–93
Methodist Episcopal Church, 31
Minimum wage, 50
Ministry, as greatest of professions, 162
Mission, social, of Christians, 90–91
Money power and the church, 129–33
Monopolies, 1, 51–52, 73, 138–43
Movement, co-operative, 21, 48–49
    Greatest in history, 94–95
    Labor, American, 2–3, 50–52
    Social, and the church, 20–22

Natural monopolies, 138–43
New Social Order, 27–28, 40–41
    Christian influence on, 66–70
Niebuhr, Reinhold, xxii
Northern Baptist Convention, 31, 128

Old Testament prophets, 5–10
Organized Christianity, beginnings of, 94
Owen, Robert, 26

Parkhurst, Charles H., 147
Primitive Christianity, 14–16
    Society, 23
Prohibition campaigns, 30–31
Prophets and pioneers, 158–59
Prophets of Judaism, 5–10
Protestant Episcopal Church, General Convention, 1913, 74
Protestant Reformation, 17, 143
Prayer of social Christianity, 30–36
Prayers of Social Awakening, 150–61
    Author's prayer, 161
    Of wrath, against war, 157
    For the babies, 155
    For children who work, 152
    For the co-operative commonwealth, 160
    For employers, 153
    For the Fatherhood of God, 150
    For the Kingdom of God, 157–58
    For ministers, 154
    For our city, 159
    For prophets and pioneers, 158–59
    For writers and newspapermen, 154

For women who toil, 152–53
For this world, 151
Morituri te salutant, 156
Pulpit and social reform, 145–47

Race relations, 126
Rauschenbusch, Walter, life and work, xiii–xxii
  Chronology, 163
  Influence of, xvi–xviii, 39–104
  Letter to one entering ministry, 162
  Prayers written by, 150–61
Revolution, industrial, 18–19
  Social, of the west, 4–5
Regeneration of social life, 99
Revival of Religion, 62–72
Riis, Jacob, xvii, 27
Rochester Theological Seminary, xvii
Roman Catholic Church, 60
  Federations of labor, 54
Roosevelt, Theodore, viii, xxi, 1, 27, 30, 37, 38, 128
  On socialism, xxi, 55

Sanitation of the wealthy classes, 69
Second German Baptist Church, New York, 2
Self-help *vs.* state help, 135–37
Shaftesbury, Lord, 63–64, 71
Sharpe, Dores Robinson, viii, 32, 38–39
Sin and society, 109–11
  Corporate aspects of, 110
Sin of organized economic groups, 109–10
Single tax, xviii, 52–53, 142
Smith, Gerald B., 107
Social action advocated, 22–29
Social Christianity, spread of, 32
Social gospel elaborated, 102–27
  Challenge to theology, 104–11
  Since Rauschenbusch, 103

Social gospel since Rauschenbusch, xvi–xviii, 3, 39, 104
Social justice, championship of, 26
Social mission of Christians, 20–29, 90–91
Social movement and the church, 20–22
Social order, new, 27–28, 40–41
  Christian influence on, 66–70
Social principles taught by Jesus, 89–101
Social reform and the pulpit, 145–47
Social revolution, western, 4
  Relation of Christianity to, 5
Social suffering and healing, 125
  Unjust suffering, 123
Socialism, xx, xxi, 46, 54–61, 136–37
  Christian, xx
Southern Baptist Convention, 128
State and church, 143–45
Stebbins, Henry H., 31
Stewardship, individual *vs.* social, 45, 70–71
Strayer, Paul Moore, 31
Strong, Josiah, xvii, 105
Students, outlines for, 100–101
Student Volunteers, 72
Suffering, Christian explanations of, 123–24
Sunday, Billy, 89
Sun Yat Sen, 64

Taylor Foundation lectures, 104
Temperance teaching by churches, 2, 30–31
Theology, and social gospel, 102–27
  Handicap to social gospel, 108
Todt, Rudolf, 26
Tolstoy, Leo, 69

Wilson, Woodrow, 38, 73, 109
World War I, entry of U. S. into, 102

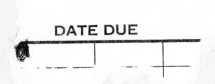

DATE DUE